Southern Barbecued Pork on a Bun (page 300)

Ginger Pork Wraps (page 301)

Oktoberfest Hot Potato Salad (page 325)

Rhubarb Blueberry Pudding Cake (page 340)

Double Berry Maple Crumble (page 345)

Baked Lemon Sponge (page 352)

Double Chocolate Caramel Bread Pudding (page 363)

Pork Chops with Mixed Winter Fruit

Pork and dried fruit were made for one another, and here's the dish that proves it.

• • •

Tip
Packages of mixed dried fruit are available in the supermarket — or you can make your own mix of apples, peaches, pears, apricots and prunes. Make sure you use whole pieces of dried fruit.

• • •

Variation
Try using apricot nectar or apple juice instead of the orange juice. The resulting flavors will be different, but just as deliciously sweet.

● **Slow cooker size: 3½ to 6 quart**

2 tsp	vegetable oil	10 mL
4	pork loin rib end chops or shoulder butt chops, 1 inch (2.5 cm) thick, trimmed of excess fat	4
1 cup	orange juice	250 mL
1 tsp	Worcestershire sauce	5 mL
½ tsp	ground ginger	2 mL
½ tsp	ground allspice	2 mL
½ tsp	ground cinnamon	2 mL
1	package (12 oz/375 g) dried mixed fruit	1

1. In a skillet, heat oil over medium-high heat. Add pork chops in batches and cook for 5 minutes per side, or until browned. Remove pork and pat dry with paper towels to remove any excess oil.

2. Place pork chops in slow cooker stoneware. Add orange juice, Worcestershire sauce, ginger, allspice, cinnamon and dried fruit.

3. Cover and cook on **Low** for 7 to 9 hours or on **High** for 3 to 4 hours, until meat is tender. Serve pork chops with fruit spooned over top.

Pork Chops with Spiced Fruit Stuffing

Using store-bought dry stuffing mix makes this dish a snap to prepare. Who would believe you could eat something this good during the week?

• • •

Tip
You can also use shoulder butt chops in this recipe. If so, cook on Low for 6 to 8 hours or on High for 3 to 4 hours, and reduce the chicken broth by ¼ cup (50 mL), since these pork chops tend to release more juices when slow-cooked. This will ensure that the stuffing does not become too soggy.

• **Slow cooker size: 3½ to 6 quart**

1 tbsp	vegetable oil	15 mL
4 to 6	boneless pork loin rib end chops, 1 inch (2.5 cm) thick, trimmed of excess fat	4 to 6
⅓ cup	raisins	75 mL
⅓ cup	dried cranberries	75 mL
⅓ cup	chopped dried apricots	75 mL
¼ tsp	salt	1 mL
Pinch	freshly ground black pepper	Pinch
½ cup	apple juice, divided	125 mL
1 cup	chicken stock	250 mL
2 tbsp	butter	25 mL
¼ tsp	ground cinnamon	1 mL
Pinch	ground nutmeg	Pinch
1	package (6 oz/175 g) herb-seasoned stuffing mix	1

1. In a large nonstick skillet, heat oil over medium-high heat. Cook pork chops in batches for about 5 minutes per side, or until browned.

2. Transfer pork to slow cooker stoneware. Sprinkle with raisins, cranberries, apricots, salt, pepper and ¼ cup (50 mL) apple juice.

3. In a saucepan, combine remaining ¼ cup (50 mL) apple juice, stock, butter, cinnamon and nutmeg. Bring to a boil and stir in dry stuffing and seasoning pouch mix. Remove from heat and spoon over fruit in slow cooker.

4. Cover and cook on **Low** for 4 to 5 hours or on **High** for 2 to 3 hours, until pork is tender and just a hint of pink remains.

5. To serve, scoop out stuffing and fruit and place in a bowl. Stir gently. Serve with pork chops.

Country-Style Honey Garlic Ribs

These sweet and tangy ribs are always a party hit. Have lots of napkins on hand for sticky fingers.

• • •

Tips

For added flavor, combine broiled ribs and sauce in a large bowl and marinate in the refrigerator for 1 hour. Transfer to slow cooker and proceed with Step 3.

To feed a larger (or hungrier!) crowd, double sauce ingredients and add 5 to 6 lbs (2.5 to 3 kg) ribs, cut into 2-rib portions.

Country-style ribs are the meatiest variety of pork ribs, but ordinary side ribs will also work in this recipe. To tenderize, cut ribs into 5- or 6-rib pieces and place in a large pot of water. Bring to a boil, reduce heat and simmer for 30 to 45 minutes.

● Slow cooker size: 3½ to 5 quart

3 lbs	country-style pork ribs, cut into individual ribs	1.5 kg
	Freshly ground black pepper	
1 cup	barbecue sauce (preferably smoke-flavored)	250 mL
½ cup	liquid honey	125 mL
¼ cup	red wine vinegar	50 mL
4	cloves garlic, minced	4

1. Position a broiler rack 6 inches (15 cm) from heat source and preheat broiler. Place ribs on foil-lined broiler pan or baking sheet and season well with pepper. Broil ribs, turning once, for 15 minutes or until browned. Drain and place ribs in slow cooker stoneware.

2. In a bowl, combine barbecue sauce, honey, vinegar and garlic; stir well. Pour sauce over ribs in slow cooker.

3. Cover and cook, stirring ribs twice during cooking to coat well, on **Low** for 8 to 10 hours or on **High** for 4 to 6 hours, until ribs are tender and browned in sauce.

Key West Ribs

For a taste of the tropics in the middle of winter, make a batch of these meaty ribs.

• • •

Tips

Country-style ribs are the meatiest variety of pork ribs. They are cut from the loin, so they tend to have less fat than side or back ribs. If you can't find country-style ribs, side or back ribs will also work in this recipe. Broil them for 8 to 10 minutes on each side before placing them in the slow cooker.

A quick way to mix cornstarch with a liquid is to use a jar. Screw the lid on tightly and shake the jar until the mixture is smooth. (This is faster than trying to stir or whisk until all the cornstarch is dissolved.)

● **Slow cooker size: 3 ½ to 6 quart**

3 lbs	country-style pork ribs, cut into individual ribs	1.5 kg
1	onion, finely chopped	1
¼ cup	barbecue sauce	50 mL
1 tsp	grated orange zest	5 mL
1 tsp	grated lime zest	5 mL
	Juice of 1 orange (about ¼ cup/50 mL)	
	Juice of 1 lime (about 2 tbsp/25 mL)	
2 tbsp	cornstarch	25 mL
2 tbsp	cold water	25 mL
	Salt and freshly ground black pepper	

1. Place ribs on a foil-lined broiler pan or baking sheet. Place about 6 inches (15 cm) from preheated broiler element. Broil, turning often, for 10 to 15 minutes, or until browned on all sides. Transfer to a paper towel–lined plate to drain. Transfer to slow cooker stoneware.

2. In a bowl, combine onion, barbecue sauce, orange and lime zest and orange and lime juice. Pour over ribs.

3. Cover and cook on **Low** for 6 to 8 hours or on **High** for 3 to 4 hours, until ribs are tender.

4. Transfer ribs to a platter and keep warm. Skim fat from sauce.

5. In a small bowl or jar, dissolve cornstarch in cold water (see tip, at left) and whisk into sauce. Cover and cook on **High** for 10 minutes, or until thickened. Season with salt and pepper.

Slow and Easy Barbecued Ribs

While many of us think of a grill as a barbecue, those in the Carolinas know that an authentic barbecue means slow-cooking pork with a "mop," or top-secret sauce, over a smoldering fire. This recipe uses the same principle and cooks meaty ribs slowly in a rich, savory barbecue sauce.

• • •

Tip
Serve with coleslaw (page 115), pickles and cornbread.

● Slow cooker size: 3 ½ to 6 quart

3 lbs	country-style pork ribs, cut into individual ribs	1.5 kg
1	large onion, chopped	1
½ cup	finely chopped celery	125 mL
¾ cup	ketchup	175 mL
¼ cup	apple juice	50 mL
¼ cup	water	50 mL
2 tbsp	freshly squeezed lemon juice	25 mL
2 tbsp	packed brown sugar	25 mL
1 tbsp	dry mustard	15 mL
1 tbsp	cider vinegar	15 mL
1 tbsp	Worcestershire sauce	15 mL
2 tsp	paprika	10 mL
1 tbsp	prepared horseradish	15 mL

1. Place ribs on a foil-lined broiler pan or baking sheet. Place 6 inches (15 cm) from preheated broiler element. Broil, turning often, for 10 to 15 minutes, or until browned on all sides. Transfer to a paper towel–lined plate to drain. Transfer ribs to slow cooker stoneware.

2. In a bowl, combine onion, celery, ketchup, apple juice, water, lemon juice, brown sugar, dry mustard, vinegar, Worcestershire sauce and paprika. Pour sauce over ribs.

3. Cover and cook on **Low** for 6 to 8 hours or on **High** for 3 to 4 hours, until ribs are tender.

4. Transfer ribs to a serving platter and keep warm. Skim fat from sauce and stir in horseradish.

5. For a thicker sauce, transfer to a saucepan and bring to a boil. Simmer gently, stirring often, until sauce is desired consistency. Serve sauce over ribs or on the side for dipping.

Slow Cooker-to-Grill Sticky Ribs

<table>
<tr><td colspan="2">**Serves 4**</td></tr>
</table>

This is a great way to use your slow cooker in the hot summer months, without heating up the kitchen.

Make Ahead

Prepare these succulent ribs the night before and let them cook in the slow cooker while you are sleeping. Refrigerate the ribs the next morning in the sticky sauce. They will be ready to throw on the grill at the end of the day.

● Slow cooker size: 3½ to 6 quart

4 lbs	pork back ribs, trimmed of excess fat, cut into serving-sized portions	2 kg
1	onion, sliced	1
1	stalk celery, with leaves	1
2	cloves garlic, peeled and crushed	2
2	bay leaves	2
1 tsp	whole black peppercorns	5 mL

Sticky Sauce

½ cup	barbecue sauce	125 mL
½ cup	grape jelly	125 mL
2	cloves garlic, minced	2
Dash	hot pepper sauce	Dash

1. Place ribs in slow cooker stoneware. (For smaller slow cookers, ribs may have to be cut into smaller portions to fit.)

2. Place onion, celery, garlic, bay leaves and peppercorns around ribs. Cover with water.

3. Cover and cook on **Low** for 6 to 8 hours, or until ribs are tender. Transfer ribs to a bowl. Discard cooking liquid and vegetables.

4. *Sticky sauce:* In a saucepan over medium heat, combine barbecue sauce, grape jelly, minced garlic and hot pepper sauce. Cook for 5 minutes, stirring constantly, until jelly has melted.

5. Preheat barbecue and carefully oil grill rack. Brush ribs generously with sauce. Grill ribs over low heat 4 to 6 inches (10 to 15 cm) from coals. Grill for 15 to 20 minutes, or until browned, turning occasionally and brushing with sauce. Discard any remaining sauce.

Slow Cooker Cottage Roll

	Serves 8	

Tip

A cottage roll is the top end of the pork shoulder (otherwise known as the shoulder butt) and is cured in a brine. Its flavor is very similar to ham — but it is much less expensive. It is just the right size for a slow cooker and available at most supermarkets in Canada — although not, unfortunately, in America. If you can't find a cottage roll, use ham instead.

● Slow cooker size: 3½ to 5 quart

1	pickled pork cottage roll or smoked ham (3 to 3½ lbs/1.5 to 1.6 kg)	1
6	peppercorns	6
1	bay leaf	1
1	stalk celery, chopped	1
1	potato, peeled and diced	1
	Ginger ale or water	
	Grainy mustard	

1. If using cottage roll, remove plastic wrap (but not elastic string) and rinse to remove brine. Place cottage roll or ham in slow cooker stoneware. Add peppercorns, bay leaf, celery and potato. Add ginger ale to within 1 inch (2.5 cm) of top of slow cooker.

2. Cover and cook on **Low** for 8 to 10 hours or on **High** for 4 to 6 hours, until meat is tender and completely cooked.

3. Remove meat from slow cooker. Strain cooking liquid, discarding vegetables and seasonings. (Liquid can be used for making Black Bean Cassoulet Soup; see recipe, page 104.) Slice meat and serve with your favorite grainy mustard.

Winter Root and Sausage Casserole

For a chill-chasing menu, serve this hearty casserole with thick slices of warm pumpernickel bread and mugs of hot orange-spice tea.

Make Ahead

Casserole can be assembled 12 hours in advance. Prepare the ingredients in the slow cooker up to the cooking stage (without adding parsley) and refrigerate in stoneware insert overnight. The next day, place stone-ware in slow cooker and continue cooking as directed.

● Slow cooker size: 3½ to 6 quart

1	large potato, peeled and cut into ½-inch (1 cm) cubes	1
1	large sweet potato, peeled and cut into ½-inch (1 cm) cubes	1
2	carrots, peeled and coarsely chopped	2
1	parsnip, peeled and coarsely chopped	1
1	onion, finely chopped	1
1 lb	smoked sausages, sliced	500 g
1	can (19 oz/540 mL) Italian-style stewed tomatoes, with juices (see box, page 97)	1
1½ cups	chicken stock	375 mL
2 tsp	granulated sugar	10 mL
½ tsp	dried thyme	2 mL
¼ tsp	freshly ground black pepper	1 mL
¼ cup	chopped fresh parsley	50 mL

1. In slow cooker stoneware, combine potato, sweet potato, carrots, parsnip, onion, sausages, tomatoes (with juices), stock, sugar, thyme and pepper; stir to mix well.

2. Cover and cook on **Low** for 7 to 9 hours or on **High** for 3 to 4 hours, until vegetables are tender.

3. Stir in parsley during last 10 to 15 minutes of cooking time.

Parsnips

Parsnips are a wonderful winter vegetable that resemble white carrots. (At least that's the description I give my vegetable-wary children when they ask, "What's that?") Parsnips have a slightly sweet flavor and make a delicious addition to many soups and stews.

Tourtière Shepherd's Pie

This is a perfect dish to turn on before heading out the door to Christmas Eve mass.

• • •

Tip

Serve with a crisp salad of garden greens and chili sauce. (If you make this in a larger slow cooker, the pie will be thinner, but the yield will be the same.)

Make Ahead

This dish can be assembled up to 24 hours before cooking. Cook meat and vegetables and chill separately before assembling in slow cooker. Refrigerate overnight in the slow cooker stoneware. The next day, place stoneware in slow cooker and continue to cook as directed.

● **Slow cooker size: 3½ to 6 quart**

6	potatoes, peeled and cut into ¾-inch (2 cm) cubes	6
2 lbs	lean ground pork, chicken or turkey	1 kg
1 tbsp	vegetable oil	15 mL
2	onions, finely chopped	2
5	cloves garlic, minced	5
1	stalk celery, finely chopped	1
1½ tsp	dried thyme	7 mL
½ tsp	dried savory	2 mL
½ tsp	salt	2 mL
½ tsp	freshly ground black pepper	2 mL
¼ tsp	ground cloves	1 mL
¼ tsp	ground cinnamon	1 mL
1 cup	chicken stock	250 mL
2 tbsp	chopped fresh parsley	25 mL

1. Cook potatoes in a pot of boiling salted water until tender, about 15 minutes. With a slotted spoon, transfer 1½ cups (375 mL) potatoes to lightly greased slow cooker stoneware. Drain remaining potatoes and return to pot. Mash until smooth and set aside.

2. In a large nonstick skillet, over medium-high heat, cook pork, breaking up with back of a spoon, until no longer pink. Drain and place in slow cooker stoneware.

3. Add oil to pan and heat. Add onions, garlic and celery. Cook, stirring occasionally, for 5 minutes, or until softened. Add thyme, savory, salt, pepper, cloves and cinnamon. Cook, stirring, for 1 minute, or until fragrant. Add to meat in slow cooker along with stock and parsley. Stir to combine.

4. Spread reserved mashed potatoes over top of meat mixture.

5. Cover and cook on **Low** for 6 to 10 hours or on **High** for 3 to 4 hours, until bubbling and heated through.

Pulled Pork Fajitas

Even though this pork never comes within spitting distance of a glowing ember, the flavor is that of your classic Carolinian barbecued pork sandwich.

• • •

Tips

Leftover pulled (shredded) pork can be stored in the refrigerator for up to 4 days or frozen for up to 4 months and used in tacos, enchiladas and burritos.

You can use a boneless beef cross rib or rump roast or 2 lbs (1 kg) skinless turkey thighs in place of the pork.

● Slow cooker size: 3½ to 6 quart

1	boneless pork shoulder butt roast (about 3 lbs/1.5 kg), trimmed of excess fat	1
1	onion, chopped	1
1 cup	ketchup	250 mL
¾ cup	salsa	175 mL
¾ cup	cola	175 mL
¼ cup	packed brown sugar	50 mL
2 tbsp	rice vinegar	25 mL
4	cloves garlic, minced	4
1 tsp	liquid smoke (see tip, page 275)	5 mL
1 tsp	hot pepper flakes	5 mL
8 to 12	10-inch (25 cm) flour tortillas	8 to 12

1. Place pork in slow cooker stoneware and sprinkle onion over top.

2. In a large bowl, combine ketchup, salsa, cola, brown sugar, vinegar, garlic, liquid smoke and hot pepper flakes. Pour over pork in slow cooker.

3. Cover and cook on **Low** for 10 to 12 hours or on **High** for 5 to 6 hours, until pork is very tender.

4. Transfer pork to a large bowl and, using two forks, pull meat into shreds. Skim fat from sauce. Return meat to sauce to keep warm.

5. Wrap tortillas in foil and warm in a preheated 350°F (180°C) oven for 10 minutes. When ready to serve, spoon filling onto warm tortillas and roll up.

Double-Decker Spicy Pork Tacos

Tacos are Mexican-style sandwiches filled with meat, beans, cheese, lettuce, onions, salsa and guacamole. In this recipe, soft flour tortillas prevent the filling from falling out of the crispy taco shells — a common hazard when you are eating tacos! Add any extra toppings you wish.

● **Slow cooker size: 3 1/2 to 6 quart**

1	boneless pork loin rib end roast (about 2 lbs/1 kg), trimmed of excess fat	1
1 tbsp	chili powder	15 mL
1/4 tsp	ground cumin	1 mL
1/4 tsp	hot pepper flakes	1 mL
1	can (19 oz/540 mL) tomatoes, drained and chopped	1
1	can (4 1/2 oz/127 mL) chopped mild green chilies, including liquid	1
1	can (14 oz/398 mL) refried beans	1
12	6-inch (15 cm) flour tortillas	12
12	taco shells	12
3/4 cup	shredded Cheddar cheese	175 mL
1 1/2 cups	shredded lettuce	375 mL

1. Place pork roast in slow cooker stoneware. Sprinkle chili powder, cumin and hot pepper flakes over roast. Add tomatoes and green chilies.

2. Cover and cook on **Low** for 8 to 10 hours or on **High** for 4 to 5 hours, until pork is tender.

3. Transfer pork to a bowl and, using two forks, pull meat into shreds. Skim fat from sauce. Return meat to sauce in slow cooker.

4. Heat refried beans, tortillas and taco shells according to package directions.

5. Spread flour tortillas with a spoonful of hot refried beans. Set 1 taco shell in center. Fold flour tortilla around taco shell. Spoon about 1/3 cup (75 mL) pork mixture into each taco shell. Top with cheese and lettuce.

Southern Barbecued Pork on a Bun

This is perfect picnic fare — easy to make ahead (see below) and serve to appreciative family and friends in the great outdoors.

Make Ahead

Marinate the pork up to 24 hours in advance. Cook meat overnight in slow cooker, slice, then return it to the warm sauce. Wrap the removable insert with towels and secure lid with elastic bands, then pack in a tight box. Take to the picnic and serve immediately.

● Slow cooker size: 3½ to 5 quart

1 cup	ketchup	250 mL
1 cup	chili sauce (homemade or store-bought)	250 mL
¼ cup	Dijon mustard	50 mL
2 tbsp	cider vinegar or white vinegar	25 mL
1 tbsp	Worcestershire sauce	15 mL
½ tsp	hot pepper flakes	2 mL
4	cloves garlic, minced	4
1	boneless pork shoulder butt roast (about 3 lbs/1.5 kg), trimmed of excess fat	1
8	kaiser buns, split	8

1. In a saucepan, over medium-high heat, combine ketchup, chili sauce, mustard, vinegar, Worcestershire sauce, hot pepper flakes and garlic. Bring mixture to a boil, reduce heat and simmer for 5 minutes. Let cool.

2. Place roast in a large glass bowl or resealable plastic bag. Pour sauce over pork and marinate overnight in the refrigerator.

3. Remove roast from marinade and place in slow cooker stoneware. Add ¾ cup (175 mL) water to marinade; mix well and add to roast in slow cooker.

4. Cover and cook on **Low** for 8 to 10 hours or on **High** for 4 to 6 hours, until meat is tender.

5. Remove meat from barbecue sauce and let stand 10 to 15 minutes before carving into thin slices. Place meat on one half of kaiser bun, add additional barbecue sauce and top with other half of bun.

Ginger Pork Wraps

These wraps combine the flavors of sweet-and-sour pork with crisp vegetables. Everyone will be asking for seconds.

• • •

Tip

If you are pressed for time, look for pre-packaged coleslaw mix to use in place of the cabbage and carrot (use about 3½ cups/875 mL).

● Slow cooker size: 3½ to 6 quart

¼ cup	hoisin sauce	50 mL
3 tbsp	grated gingerroot	45 mL
3 tbsp	liquid honey	45 mL
1	boneless pork loin rib end roast (about 2½ lbs/1.25 kg), trimmed of excess fat	1
2½ cups	shredded cabbage	625 mL
½ cup	shredded carrot	125 mL
3	green onions, finely chopped	3
2 tbsp	rice vinegar	25 mL
10 to 12	10-inch (25 cm) flour tortillas	10 to 12

1. In a bowl, combine hoisin sauce, ginger and honey.
2. Place pork roast in slow cooker stoneware and brush with sauce to coat completely.
3. Cover and cook on **Low** for 8 to 10 hours or on **High** for 4 to 5 hours, until meat is very tender.
4. Transfer pork to a bowl and, using two forks, pull meat into shreds. Skim fat from sauce. Return meat to slow cooker.
5. In a bowl, combine cabbage, carrot, green onions and vinegar.
6. Wrap tortillas in foil and heat in a preheated 350°F (180°C) oven for 10 minutes. To serve, spread about ⅓ cup (75 mL) pork mixture down center of each warm tortilla. Top with ¼ cup (50 mL) cabbage mixture. Roll up each tortilla tightly.

Fresh Gingerroot

There is no need to peel gingerroot before grating. Use a standard kitchen grater with fine holes. Wrap any unused ginger in plastic wrap and freeze. Frozen gingerroot can be grated without defrosting.

Lamb Shanks with Braised Beans

In this version of a classic French recipe, economical lamb shanks are cooked slowly in a savory sauce, becoming extremely tender and flavorful.

• • •

Tips

Parsnips are a wonderful winter vegetable that resemble white carrots. (At least that's the description I give my vegetable-wary children when they ask, "What's that?") Parsnips have a slightly sweet flavor and make a delicious addition to many soups and stews.

Tired of opening a whole can of tomato paste when all you need is a small amount? Look for the squeeze tubes of tomato paste sold in most supermarkets.

Be sure to crumble the rosemary between your fingers before adding it to the marinade. This helps to release the full aromatic flavor of the herb.

● Slow cooker size: 5 to 6 quart

1 tbsp	vegetable oil	15 mL
4	meaty lamb shanks (2 to 3 lbs/1 to 1.5 kg total)	4
1 tsp	salt	5 mL
½ tsp	freshly ground black pepper	2 mL
1	can (19 oz/540 mL) white beans, drained and rinsed, or 2 cups (500 mL) home-cooked beans (page 146)	1
2	parsnips, peeled and cut into 1-inch (2.5 cm) chunks	2
2	carrots, peeled and cut into 1-inch (2.5 cm) chunks	2
1	onion, quartered	1
½ cup	dry red wine	125 mL
½ cup	chicken stock	125 mL
2 tbsp	tomato paste	25 mL
4	cloves garlic, peeled and halved	4
2 tbsp	finely chopped parsley	25 mL
2 tsp	dried rosemary, crumbled	10 mL
1	bay leaf	1
1 tbsp	chopped fresh parsley	15 mL

1. In a large nonstick skillet, heat oil over medium-high heat. In batches, cook lamb shanks for about 5 to 7 minutes per side, or until brown. Season with salt and pepper.

2. Place beans, parsnips, carrots and onion in slow cooker stoneware. Place browned lamb shanks on top of bean-vegetable mixture.

3. In a bowl, combine wine, stock and tomato paste. Pour over meat and vegetables. Sprinkle with garlic, parsley, rosemary and bay leaf.

4. Cover and cook on **Low** for 8 to 12 hours or on **High** for 4 to 5 hours, until lamb is very tender and falling off the bones.

5. With a slotted spoon, transfer meat, beans and vegetables to a platter, cover and keep warm. Discard bay leaf.

6. Skim fat from pan juices and transfer liquid to a saucepan. Boil for 10 minutes to thicken. Spoon juices over meat, beans and vegetables. Garnish with parsley.

Tip

Serve garnished with chopped fresh parsley and accompanied by garlic mashed potatoes to soak up the juices.

Garlic Mashed Potatoes

Peel 2 lbs (1 kg) potatoes and cut into quarters. Place potatoes in a saucepan and cover with water. Add 1 tsp (5 mL) salt. Bring to a boil, cover and reduce heat to medium. Boil gently for 20 to 30 minutes, or until tender. Drain well and return to saucepan.

In a separate small saucepan, heat 1/4 cup (50 mL) butter over medium heat. Add 2 cloves peeled and crushed garlic and cook for 5 minutes, or until fragrant. Add 1 cup (250 mL) milk, 1/2 tsp (2 mL) salt and 1/2 tsp (2 mL) black pepper, and heat until milk is hot.

Pour into saucepan with potatoes and mash until smooth. Taste and adjust seasonings if necessary. *Makes 4 servings.*

Calcutta Lamb Curry

Accompany this sweet and flavorful curry with additional sweet mango chutney and a selection of condiments — chopped green onions, chopped peanuts and toasted coconut. It's best served on a bed of sweet-scented basmati, a long-grain East Indian rice.

• • •

Tips

Mango chutney is found in the condiment section of most supermarkets.

Canned coconut milk is made from grated and soaked coconut pulp — not, as you might think, from the liquid found inside the coconut. It can be found in the Asian foods section of most supermarkets or Asian food stores. Be sure you don't buy coconut cream, which is often used for making tropical drinks such as piña coladas, and is far too sweet for curry.

● **Slow cooker size: 3½ to 5 quart**

2 tbsp	vegetable oil (approx.)	25 mL
1	lamb shank or butt roast (about 2 lbs/1 kg), well trimmed and cut into 1-inch (2.5 cm) cubes	1
2 tbsp	all-purpose flour	25 mL
2 tbsp	curry powder	25 mL
½ tsp	hot pepper flakes	2 mL
½ tsp	paprika	2 mL
½ tsp	dried marjoram	2 mL
1 cup	chicken stock	250 mL
2	large Granny Smith apples, peeled and coarsely chopped	2
2	stalks celery, coarsely chopped	2
2	onions, finely chopped	2
2	cloves garlic, minced	2
1 tbsp	minced gingerroot	15 mL
1	can (14 oz/398 mL) coconut milk	1
1 tsp	salt	5 mL
¼ cup	mango chutney	50 mL
½ cup	raisins	125 mL
⅓ cup	plain yogurt or sour cream	75 mL
1 tsp	grated lemon zest	5 mL

1. In a large nonstick skillet, heat half the oil over medium-high heat. Cook lamb in batches, adding more oil as needed, until browned all over. Return all lamb to skillet.

2. In a small bowl, combine flour, curry powder, hot pepper flakes, paprika and marjoram. Sprinkle over lamb cubes, tossing to coat well. Add stock and cook, scraping up brown bits from bottom of skillet. Bring to a boil, reduce heat and simmer for about 5 minutes.

3. Transfer meat mixture to slow cooker stoneware. Add apples, celery, onions, garlic, ginger, coconut milk and salt.

4. Cover and cook on **Low** for 8 to 10 hours or on **High** for 4 to 6 hours, until meat is tender.

5. Transfer curry to a serving dish. Stir in chutney, raisins, yogurt and lemon zest. Serve immediately.

Curry Powder

Curry powder, a blend of more than 20 herbs, seeds and spices, is integral to Indian cuisine (in India, most cooks blend their own mixtures). Cardamom, chilies, cinnamon, coriander, cumin, fennel, mace, pepper, poppy and sesame seeds and saffron are common curry seasonings. Turmeric gives curry its distinctive yellow color.

Curry paste can be used instead of curry powder. It comes in different heat levels, so buy a mild version if you don't like your curry too hot.

To eliminate the raw taste of curry powder and sweeten the spice, sauté it in a dry skillet before using. Cook for about 30 seconds, or just until fragrant.

Make Ahead

This dish can be assembled up to 12 hours in advance. Prepare the ingredients as directed up to the cooking stage, (but without adding chutney, raisins and lemon zest), and refrigerate in stoneware insert overnight. The next day, place stone-ware in slow cooker and continue cooking as directed.

Rosemary and Garlic Leg of Lamb

Serves 6 to 8

This recipe takes its inspiration from the Greek isles. The rub-on paste infuses the lamb as it cooks, making the meat fragrant with garlic, lemon and herbs. Slow-roasting this cut ensures juicy, tender results.

• • •

Tip
Remember to remove the string from the roast before carving and serving.

● Slow cooker size: 6 quart

6	cloves garlic, peeled and crushed	6
	Grated zest of 1 lemon	
1 tbsp	chopped fresh rosemary (or 1 tsp/5 mL dried)	15 mL
1 tsp	salt	5 mL
½ tsp	freshly ground black pepper	2 mL
1	boneless leg of lamb (3 to 4 lbs/ 1.5 to 2 kg), tied	1
2 tbsp	olive oil	25 mL
½ cup	dry white wine	125 mL

1. In a small bowl or food processor, mash or chop garlic, lemon zest, rosemary, salt and pepper to form a paste. Rub all over lamb.

2. In a large nonstick skillet, heat oil over medium-high heat. Add lamb and cook, turning with tongs or two wooden spoons, for 10 minutes, or until browned on all sides. Transfer to slow cooker stoneware.

3. Pour wine into skillet and bring to a boil, scraping to remove any bits from bottom of pan. Pour over meat in slow cooker.

4. Cover and cook on **Low** for 4 to 6 hours, or until meat is tender and cooked to desired doneness.

Checking for Doneness

Use a meat thermometer to test larger cuts of meat for doneness. Roasts continue to cook for 5 to 15 minutes after they are removed from the slow cooker.
- **Rare:** 140°F (60°C)
- **Medium:** 160°F (71°C)
- **Well Done:** 170°F (77°C)

Greek Lamb Loaf with Tzatziki Sauce

Serves 4

Tip

If you're pressed for time, buy pre-made tzatziki sauce; otherwise, prepare the sauce in this recipe right after you put the loaf in the slow cooker. As the loaf cooks, let the sauce sit, covered, in the refrigerator so it can develop its flavors.

Make Ahead

This dish can be completely assembled up to 12 hours in advance of cooking. Follow preparation directions and refrigerate overnight in the slow cooker stoneware. The next day, place stoneware in slow cooker and continue cooking as directed.

● Slow cooker size: 3½ to 5 quart

2 lbs	ground lamb	1 kg
½ cup	fine dry bread crumbs	125 mL
1	onion, finely chopped	1
2	cloves garlic, minced	2
½ cup	plain yogurt	125 mL
1 tbsp	freshly squeezed lime juice	15 mL
1 tsp	each ground coriander and cumin	5 mL
½ tsp	each hot pepper flakes and salt	2 mL
1	egg, lightly beaten	1

Tzatziki Sauce

1 cup	plain yogurt	250 mL
2	cloves garlic, minced	2
1 tsp	freshly ground black pepper	5 mL
1 tsp	chopped fresh mint	5 mL

1. Cut a 2-foot (60 cm) length of foil in half lengthwise. Fold each strip in half lengthwise, forming two long strips. Crisscross the strips in the bottom of the slow cooker, bringing the ends of the foil strips up and clear of the stoneware rim.

2. In a large bowl, combine lamb, bread crumbs, onion, garlic, yogurt, lime juice, coriander, cumin, hot pepper flakes, salt and egg; mix well. Press evenly into foil-lined slow cooker stoneware, tucking foil ends under lid.

3. Cover and cook on **Low** for 8 to 10 hours or on **High** for 4 to 6 hours, or until a meat thermometer inserted into meatloaf reads 170°F (77°C). Remove lid and grasp ends of foil strips to lift out meatloaf. Let stand for 5 minutes before slicing.

4. *Tzatziki sauce:* In a bowl, combine yogurt, garlic, pepper and mint; mix well. Refrigerate for at least 2 hours, then drizzle over loaf and serve.

Side Dishes

Lisa's Classic Green Beans

My friend Lisa Wilson (who claims she is not much of a cook, though she is a good lawyer) always brings the best vegetable side dishes to our potluck dinners. While the original recipe contained canned green beans, Lisa updated it by using frozen French-cut beans. A can of condensed mushroom soup is used because it stands up well during the long cooking time.

• • •

Tips

If you can't find French-cut frozen green beans, regular-cut frozen beans can be substituted (fresh beans tend not to work as well in this recipe).

To toast almonds: Spread on a baking sheet and bake in a 350°F (180°C) oven for 5 to 7 minutes, or until golden brown and fragrant.

● Slow cooker size: 3½ to 6 quart

1	can (10 oz/284 mL) condensed cream of mushroom soup, undiluted	1
2 tbsp	sour cream	25 mL
½ tsp	salt	2 mL
½ tsp	freshly ground black pepper	2 mL
1 tbsp	chopped fresh parsley	15 mL
1 tsp	dried sage	5 mL
¼ tsp	ground nutmeg	1 mL
4 cups	frozen French-cut green beans, thawed	1 L
1	onion, finely chopped	1
½ cup	finely chopped roasted red pepper (see box, below)	125 mL
½ cup	slivered or sliced almonds, toasted (see tip, at left)	125 mL

1. In a bowl, whisk together soup, sour cream, salt, pepper, parsley, sage and nutmeg. Add frozen beans, onion and roasted red pepper. Toss to coat in soup mixture. Transfer to slow cooker stoneware.

2. Cover and cook on **Low** for 3 to 4 hours, or until hot and bubbling. Spoon into serving dish and sprinkle with toasted almonds.

Roasting Peppers

Roasted red peppers are available in jars or fresh in the deli section of some supermarkets. To make your own, preheat broiler and cut peppers in half, removing ribs and seeds. Place cut side down on a baking sheet. Place peppers about 6 inches (15 cm) from element and broil until skins turn black. Place peppers in a paper bag. Close bag and let peppers sweat for about 30 minutes. Peel off skins and chop as needed.

Honey-Lemon Beets

Serves 6 to 8

This simple side dish goes well with any type of roast. Or use it as a summer side dish to accompany barbecued meats and fish. By slow-cooking the peeled beets instead of boiling them, all the beet juices end up on your plate instead of going down the drain.

Make Ahead

This dish can be completely assembled up to 24 hours before cooking. Refrigerate overnight in the slow cooker stoneware. The next day, place stoneware in slow cooker and continue to cook as directed.

● Slow cooker size: 3½ to 6 quart

1 tbsp	butter	15 mL
1	onion, sliced	1
8	beets, peeled and quartered	8
2 tbsp	liquid honey	25 mL
2 tbsp	freshly squeezed lemon juice	25 mL
½ tsp	ground nutmeg	2 mL
¼ tsp	salt	1 mL
¼ tsp	freshly ground black pepper	1 mL
½ cup	vegetable stock	125 mL

1. In a skillet over medium heat, melt butter. Add onion and cook, stirring occasionally, for about 5 minutes, or until softened.
2. Place beets in slow cooker stoneware. Add cooked onion, honey, lemon juice, nutmeg, salt, pepper and stock. Stir to combine.
3. Cover and cook on **Low** for 8 to 10 hours or on **High** for 4 to 5 hours, until beets are tender.

Braised Cabbage and Raspberries

My mother assisted in the sampling of this dish and described it as "unbelievable." Perfect for the Thanksgiving or Christmas dinner table, it also goes especially well with pork roasts.

• • •

Tip

Red or green cabbage can be used to make this recipe. The juice from the raspberries will turn the green cabbage bright red and make red cabbage even more vibrant.

● Slow cooker size: 3½ to 6 quart

1	large head green or red cabbage, shredded (about 12 cups/3 L)	1
2	onions, thinly sliced	2
½ cup	dried cranberries	125 mL
2 cups	fresh raspberries (or one 10-oz/300 g package frozen unsweetened raspberries, thawed)	500 mL
¾ cup	raspberry vinegar	175 mL
¼ cup	butter, melted	50 mL
½ cup	granulated sugar	125 mL
1 tsp	salt	5 mL

1. Place cabbage, onions, cranberries and raspberries in slow cooker stoneware.
2. In a small bowl, combine vinegar, butter, sugar and salt. Pour over cabbage mixture and toss to combine.
3. Cover and cook on **Low** for 4 to 6 hours, or until cabbage is tender.

Tangy Red Cabbage with Apples

This is a great side dish for any meal, especially a chicken, pork or sausage entrée.

• • •

Tips

Don't worry about being too precise with the cooking time in this recipe — the cabbage can steam away on Low all day.

If you are using a food processor to shred the cabbage, use it also for the onions and apples; it will save you a lot of time.

Leftover cabbage can be frozen until needed. Pack in freezer-safe containers and store for up to 3 months. To reheat, microwave on High until hot.

Adjust the sugar and vinegar to suit your taste.

The vinegar not only adds flavor, but helps preserve the red color of the cabbage.

● Slow cooker size: 3½ to 6 quart

1	medium head red cabbage, shredded (about 10 cups/2.5 L)	1
2	Granny Smith apples, peeled and thinly sliced	2
1	onion, sliced	1
¼ cup	red wine vinegar	50 mL
¼ cup	packed brown sugar	50 mL
2 tbsp	butter or margarine	25 mL
½ cup	water	125 mL
1 tsp	salt	5 mL
1 tsp	celery seed	5 mL
½ tsp	freshly ground black pepper	2 mL

1. In slow cooker stoneware, toss together cabbage, apples and onion slices.

2. In a saucepan, over medium-high heat, combine vinegar, brown sugar, butter, water, salt, celery seed and pepper. Bring mixture to a boil, reduce heat and simmer for 1 minute, or until butter is melted and sugar is dissolved. Pour over cabbage mixture in slow cooker.

3. Cover and cook on **Low** for 4 to 6 hours, or until cabbage is tender.

Honey-Orange Braised Carrots

This dish is a wonderful choice to accompany holiday roast turkey or beef. To save time, use packages of whole peeled baby carrots.

• • •

Tips

You can double the quantity of carrots in this the recipe, but only increase the sauce ingredients by half since there is very little evaporation in slow cooking.

To get the most juice out of an orange, roll on the countertop, pressing down with the palm of your hand, or microwave on High for 20 seconds before squeezing. One orange should yield about 1/2 cup (125 mL) squeezed juice.

● **Slow cooker size: 3½ to 5 quart**

1 lb	peeled baby carrots	500 g
½ cup	freshly squeezed orange juice	125 mL
2 tbsp	liquid honey	25 mL
1 tbsp	melted butter or margarine	15 mL
1 tsp	ground ginger	5 mL
½ tsp	orange zest	2 mL
1 tbsp	chopped fresh parsley	15 mL
	Salt and freshly ground black pepper	

1. Place carrots in slow cooker stoneware.
2. In a 2-cup (500 mL) glass measure or bowl, combine orange juice, honey, butter, ginger and orange zest. Pour over carrots.
3. Cover and cook, stirring once, on **Low** for 6 to 8 hours or on **High** for 3 to 4 hours, until carrots are nicely glazed. Serve sprinkled with parsley and seasoned to taste with salt and pepper.

Scalloped Corn

Serves 6

This is a wonderful summertime side dish.

• • •

Tip

You can add $1/2$ cup (125 mL) shredded Cheddar cheese just before serving. Sprinkle over top of casserole, cover and cook on **High** for 5 minutes, or until melted.

• • •

Variation

Scalloped Lima Beans: Substitute frozen lima beans for the corn, or use a combination of corn and lima beans. Use 2 cups (500 mL) corn kernels and 2 cups (500 mL) frozen lima beans and chop 1 cup (250 mL) of each as directed in the recipe.

● Slow cooker size: $3\frac{1}{2}$ to 6 quart

4 cups	fresh or frozen corn kernels (thawed if frozen), divided	1 L
$1/2$ tsp	salt	2 mL
$1/2$ tsp	dried thyme	2 mL
$1/4$ tsp	freshly ground black pepper	1 mL
Pinch	ground nutmeg	Pinch
2 tbsp	butter	25 mL
1	onion, finely chopped	1
3 tbsp	all-purpose flour	45 mL
1 cup	milk	250 mL
2 tbsp	freshly grated Parmesan cheese	25 mL

1. In a blender or food processor, coarsely chop 2 cups (500 mL) corn. Place in slow cooker stoneware along with remaining 2 cups (500 mL) whole corn, salt, thyme, pepper and nutmeg.

2. In a large nonstick skillet, melt butter over medium heat. Add onion and cook, stirring occasionally, for 5 minutes, or until softened. Add flour and cook, stirring, for 1 minute. Add milk, bring mixture to a boil and cook, stirring constantly, for 1 minute, or until thickened. Stir in Parmesan cheese. Stir sauce into corn mixture and combine.

3. Cover and cook on **Low** for $3\frac{1}{2}$ to 4 hours, or until mixture is bubbly around edges.

Caramelized Onion and Apple Bake

If you like creamed onions, you'll absolutely love this luxurious dish. The secret of its extra-rich color and flavor comes from caramelizing the onions.

• • •

Tips

Serve this side dish with succulent roasted chicken or turkey, or a spectacular prime rib.

Tearless onions: Why is it that the doorbell always rings when you've got tears streaming down your face from slicing onions? To avoid this problem, put onions in the freezer for a few minutes before chopping.

To toast almonds: Spread onto a baking sheet and bake in a 350°F (180°C) oven, stirring once or twice, for 7 to 8 minutes, or until lightly brown and fragrant. Remove from heat and allow to cool completely.

● **Slow cooker size: 4 to 6 quart**

3 tbsp	butter or margarine, divided (approx.)	45 mL
4	large onions, sliced	4
1 tbsp	granulated sugar	15 mL
8 oz	sliced mushrooms	250 g
1	Granny Smith apple, peeled and finely chopped	1
2 tbsp	all-purpose flour	25 mL
¾ cup	chicken stock	175 mL
¼ cup	light cream cheese, softened	50 mL
2 tbsp	dry sherry	25 mL
½ tsp	salt	2 mL
¼ tsp	freshly ground black pepper	1 mL
½ cup	toasted sliced almonds	125 mL
¼ tsp	paprika	1 mL

1. In a large skillet, melt 2 tbsp (25 mL) butter over medium heat. Add onions and sugar. Cover and cook, stirring occasionally, for 12 to 15 minutes, or until onions are softened and nicely colored. With a slotted spoon, remove from skillet and set aside.

2. To same skillet, add mushrooms and apple and an additional tablespoon (15 mL) butter, if necessary. Cook, stirring, for 6 to 8 minutes, or until mushrooms have softened and released their liquid. Blend in flour and then stock. Bring mixture to a boil and cook, stirring constantly, until slightly thickened. Stir in cream cheese until melted. Remove from heat. Stir in sherry, salt, pepper and reserved onions.

3. Transfer onion mixture to lightly greased slow cooker stoneware and sprinkle with toasted almonds and paprika.

4. Cover and cook on **Low** for 6 to 8 hours or on **High** for 3 to 4 hours, until set and heated through.

Rich Spinach Casserole

This casserole is a wonderful companion to any grilled meat. Use it as an alternative to potatoes.

• • •

Tips

Always choose spinach that has crisp, bright leaves and a light, fresh aroma. (If it smells like cabbage, it's too old.) Wash well, then trim the stems before using in recipes or salads.

As a time-saving alternative to fresh spinach in this recipe, substitute 3 packages (each 10 oz/ 300 g) frozen chopped spinach, thawed and squeezed dry.

Spinach can be washed, dried and torn, then wrapped loosely in paper towels and refrigerated in a sealed plastic bag for up to 2 days.

● Slow cooker size: 3½ to 4 quart

2 lbs	fresh spinach or 2 packages (each 10 oz/300 g) spinach, washed, tough stems removed	1 kg
1 cup	light or regular cottage cheese	250 mL
¼ cup	light sour cream	50 mL
3	eggs, lightly beaten	3
2 tbsp	all-purpose flour	25 mL
½ tsp	ground nutmeg	2 mL
½ tsp	salt	2 mL
1	can (10 oz/284 mL) water chestnuts, drained and finely chopped	1

1. Place spinach in a large pot of boiling salted water. Cook over high heat, stirring, just until wilted. Place spinach in a colander to drain. Squeeze out moisture by hand; wrap in a clean, dry towel and squeeze out additional moisture. Once cooled, coarsely chop spinach.

2. In a bowl, combine cottage cheese, sour cream, eggs, flour, nutmeg and salt; mix well. Stir in chopped spinach and water chestnuts. Transfer mixture to lightly greased slow cooker stoneware.

3. Cover and cook on **Low** for 4 to 6 hours or on **High** for 2 to 3 hours, until casserole is set.

Maple Pecan Squash Wedges

Serves 8 to 10

This divine side dish is destined to become a Thanksgiving dinner classic.

• • •

Tip

If you can't find butternut squash, use another winter squash, such as Hubbard or buttercup.

Make Ahead

This dish can be completely assembled up to 24 hours before cooking. Refrigerate overnight in the slow cooker stoneware. The next day, place stoneware in the slow cooker and continue to cook as directed.

● Slow cooker size: 3½ to 6 quart

1	butternut squash, about 3 lbs (1.5 kg)	1
¼ cup	maple syrup	50 mL
2 tbsp	butter, melted	25 mL
1 tsp	grated orange zest	5 mL
½ tsp	grated gingerroot	2 mL
½ tsp	salt	2 mL
½ tsp	freshly ground black pepper	2 mL
¼ cup	chopped pecans, toasted (see box, page 30)	50 mL

1. Wash squash and cut in half lengthwise, leaving outside skin on. Remove seeds and cut each half horizontally into slices 1 inch (2.5 cm) thick. Lay slices in bottom of slow cooker stoneware.

2. In a bowl, combine maple syrup, melted butter, orange zest, ginger, salt and pepper. Pour over squash slices.

3. Cover and cook on **Low** for 6 to 8 hours or on **High** for 3 to 4 hours, until slices are fork-tender. Sprinkle with pecans.

Winter Squash

Once the fall harvest season rolls around, there are many winter squash varieties to choose from. Look for types with bright orange flesh, such as Hubbard, butternut or buttercup. If you are not a squash fan, sweet potatoes are a good alternative. Some supermarkets sell fresh pre-chopped squash, which saves you the trouble of peeling.

Cider-Braised Turnips

Even if you've never been a huge fan of turnips or rutabagas, this side dish is sure to make you one. The sweet flavor of the apple cider complements the tartness of this hearty winter vegetable.

• • •

Tips

For extra sweetness, add an additional 2 tbsp (25 mL) brown sugar to the turnip and cider before cooking.

Make ahead

Turnip can be cooked in the cider a day ahead, puréed, then refrigerated until ready to use. Reheat in slow cooker on Low for 2 to 3 hours or until heated through.

● Slow cooker size: 3 ½ to 4 quart

4 cups	diced peeled turnip or rutabaga (about 2 lbs/1 kg)	1 L
2 cups	apple cider	500 mL
2 tbsp	butter or margarine	25 mL
2 tbsp	packed brown sugar	25 mL
¼ tsp	ground nutmeg	1 mL
	Salt and freshly ground black pepper	

1. In slow cooker stoneware, combine turnip and cider.

2. Cover and cook on **Low** for 8 to 10 hours or on **High** for 4 to 6 hours, until turnip is tender and most of the cider has evaporated.

3. In a bowl, with a potato masher, or in a food processor, mash or purée turnip. Add butter, brown sugar and nutmeg; mix well. Season to taste with salt and pepper. If not serving immediately, return mixture to slow cooker, cover and keep warm on **Low** until ready to serve.

Turnips

Turnips are often confused with rutabagas. Although the rutabaga is a member of the turnip family, it is large, yellow-fleshed and slightly sweeter than the turnip. In this recipe (and others), the two can be used interchangeably — and both can be stored all winter in a cold cellar. Remember to remove the waxy outer skin before cooking.

Root Vegetables in Balsamic Vinegar

Serves 4 to 6

I love the way slow braising brings out the sweet flavors of the hearty winter vegetables in this dish. It's a wonderful accompaniment to a Sunday night roast.

• • •

Tip

The finest balsamic vinegar comes from Italy, where it is aged for years in wooden barrels. Its sweet-and-sour flavor and rich, winey aroma make it superb as a salad dressing or as a splash in hearty soups and stews. In fact, "vintage" balsamic vinegar is often more expensive than wine — and Italians drink it as an after-dinner digestif.

● Slow cooker size: 3½ to 6 quart

4 to 6	potatoes, peeled and cut into 2-inch (5 cm) chunks	4 to 6
3	large carrots, peeled and chopped	3
2	large parsnips, peeled and chopped	2
2	onions, quartered	2
1 cup	vegetable or chicken stock	250 mL
¼ cup	balsamic vinegar	50 mL
2 tbsp	packed brown sugar	25 mL
½ tsp	salt	2 mL
¼ tsp	freshly ground black pepper	1 mL

1. In slow cooker stoneware, combine potatoes, carrots, parsnips and onions.
2. In a bowl, combine stock, vinegar, brown sugar, salt and pepper; mix well. Pour over vegetables in slow cooker.
3. Cover and cook, stirring once every hour, on **Low** for 8 to 10 hours or on **High** for 4 to 6 hours, until vegetables are tender.

Scalloped Sweet Potatoes and Parsnips

This delectable side dish almost outshines the turkey or ham. And there's less to fuss about when there's company and you have a standby vegetable cooking in the slow cooker. It frees up the oven for other dishes.

• • •

Tip

Parsnips are a sweet root vegetable; they look like white carrots. If you have a hard time finding them, substitute carrots.

Make Ahead

This dish can be completely assembled up to 24 hours before cooking. Refrigerate overnight in slow cooker stoneware. The next day, place stoneware in slow cooker and continue to cook as directed.

● Slow cooker size: 3½ to 6 quart

3 tbsp	butter	45 mL
2	leeks (white and light green parts only), rinsed and thinly sliced	2
3 tbsp	all-purpose flour	45 mL
1½ cups	whipping (35%) cream	375 mL
1 tsp	salt	5 mL
1 tsp	dry mustard	5 mL
½ tsp	dried thyme	2 mL
¼ tsp	freshly ground black pepper	1 mL
2	sweet potatoes, peeled and cut into ¼-inch (5 mm) slices	2
2	parsnips, peeled and cut into ¼-inch (5 mm) slices	2
2 tbsp	freshly grated Parmesan cheese	25 mL

1. In a large nonstick skillet, melt butter over medium-low heat. Add leeks and cook, stirring, for 8 to 10 minutes, or until softened. Add flour and cook, stirring constantly, for 1 minute. Slowly whisk in cream, salt, dry mustard, thyme and pepper. Increase heat to medium-high and bring to a boil. Reduce heat and cook, stirring, for about 5 minutes, or until smooth and slightly thickened.

2. Layer sweet potatoes and parsnips in lightly greased slow cooker stoneware. Pour cream sauce over top. Sprinkle with Parmesan cheese.

3. Cover and cook on **Low** for 5 to 7 hours or on **High** for 3 to 4 hours, until sweet potatoes are tender.

Sweet Potato Custard

This side dish is the perfect companion to turkey, ham or roast pork. Try it with your next Thanksgiving or Easter meal.

• • •

Tip

To grease slow cooker stoneware, use a vegetable nonstick spray. Or use cake pan grease, which is available in specialty cake-decorating or bulk-food stores.

• • •

Variation

Carrot Custard: Substitute 6 cups (1.5 L) peeled and chopped carrots for the sweet potatoes.

● Slow cooker size: 3½ to 5 quart

5 cups	chopped peeled sweet potatoes	1.25 L
2 tsp	freshly squeezed lemon juice	10 mL
2 tbsp	softened butter	25 mL
¼ cup	packed brown sugar	50 mL
1 tsp	salt	5 mL
½ tsp	paprika	2 mL
1	egg	1
¼ cup	light or regular sour cream	50 mL

1. In a pot of boiling water, cook sweet potatoes for 15 to 20 minutes, or until tender. Drain and transfer to a blender or food processor. Purée or mash sweet potatoes until smooth. Add lemon juice.

2. In a bowl, combine butter, brown sugar, salt, paprika, egg and sour cream; beat until smooth. Fold in potato purée and transfer to lightly greased slow cooker stoneware.

3. Cover and cook on **Low** for 4 to 6 hours or on **High** for 2 to 3 hours, until custard is set and slightly browned around the edges.

Cheddar Scalloped Potatoes

Serves 6

This has got to be everyone's favorite potato dish. It goes well with ham, pork, chicken or turkey. My friend (and die-hard potato lover) Kathy Shortt was my principal taste-tester for this recipe. She gave it a perfect 10!

• • •

Tip

If you don't have a blender or food processor, finely chop all ingredients for the milk sauce. Pour over potatoes and continue as directed.

Make Ahead

This dish can be prepared a day ahead. Combine liquid ingredients and pour over potato and onion slices. Cover and refrigerate for up to 24 hours. Bake as directed.

● **Slow cooker size: 4 to 6 quart**

6	potatoes, peeled and sliced	6
1	onion, sliced	1
1/4 cup	celery leaves	50 mL
1 tbsp	dried parsley	15 mL
2 tbsp	butter or margarine, melted	25 mL
1/4 cup	all-purpose flour	50 mL
1 tsp	salt	5 mL
1/2 tsp	freshly ground black pepper	2 mL
1	can (13 oz/385 mL) evaporated milk	1
1 cup	shredded Cheddar cheese	250 mL
1/2 tsp	paprika	2 mL

1. Layer potato slices and onion in lightly greased slow cooker stoneware.
2. In a blender or food processor, combine celery leaves, parsley, melted butter, flour, salt, pepper, evaporated milk and Cheddar cheese. Process for 1 minute, or until mixture is smooth. Pour over potatoes and onions; sprinkle with paprika.
3. Cover and cook on **Low** for 6 to 8 hours or on **High** for 3 to 4 hours, until potatoes are tender and heated through.

Mashed Potato Soufflé

While not a true soufflé, this dish has the same kind of light texture and is great to serve alongside roast turkey or beef. And because it's prepared in the slow cooker, it also helps to free up valuable oven space when there are plenty of other side dishes to keep warm.

• • •

Tip
The fluffiness of your mash depends on the type of potatoes used. The creamy-yellow Yukon Gold variety has a wonderful buttery flavor and makes a delicious mashed potato. Russet potatoes also work very well. Regular white potatoes, while not as flavorful, also mash well. In fact, the only type that really don't work are new potatoes, since they don't have a very high starch content.

• Slow cooker size: 3½ to 5 quart

10 to 12	potatoes, scrubbed, peeled and cut into chunks	10 to 12
⅓ cup	butter, divided	75 mL
1	package (8 oz/250 g) light or regular cream cheese, softened	1
1 cup	light or regular sour cream	250 mL
2	eggs, separated	2
1 tsp	salt	5 mL
½ tsp	freshly ground black pepper	2 mL
¼ cup	fine dry bread crumbs	50 mL

1. In a large saucepan of boiling salted water, cook potatoes for 20 minutes, or until fork-tender. Drain well and return to saucepan. Add ¼ cup (50 mL) of the butter, cream cheese, sour cream, egg yolks, salt and pepper.

2. Mash potatoes with a potato masher or with an electric mixer at low speed until smooth. (Do not use a food processor or potatoes will end up with a glue-like consistency.)

3. In another bowl, beat egg whites until stiff but not dry. Fold into potato mixture. Spoon into lightly greased slow cooker stoneware.

4. In a small bowl, combine remaining 2 tbsp (25 mL) butter and bread crumbs; mix well and sprinkle over potatoes. (Mixture can be prepared up to this point and refrigerated for 24 hours.)

5. Cover and cook on **High** for 3 to 4 hours, or until puffy and slightly brown on top. Serve immediately.

Oktoberfest Hot Potato Salad

Serves 6

Oktoberfest is an annual event in my community, and you can't visit a single festhall without being tempted by a sausage on a bun and a helping of this delicious potato dish.

• • •

Tip

The beer gives this salad a wonderful rich flavor, but if you prefer, you can substitute water.

● Slow cooker size: 3½ to 6 quart

5	large potatoes, peeled, quartered and cut into 1-inch (2.5 cm) chunks (about 2½ lbs/1.25 kg)	5
1	large onion, finely chopped	1
2	stalks celery, finely chopped	2
2 tbsp	all-purpose flour	25 mL
2 tbsp	granulated sugar	25 mL
1 tsp	salt	5 mL
½ tsp	celery seed	2 mL
¼ tsp	freshly ground black pepper	1 mL
½ cup	dark beer or water	125 mL
⅓ cup	cider vinegar	75 mL
4	slices bacon, cooked crisp and crumbled	4
2 tbsp	chopped fresh parsley	25 mL

1. Place potatoes, onion and celery in slow cooker stoneware.
2. In a small bowl, combine flour, sugar, salt, celery seed and pepper. Mix well and sprinkle over vegetables in slow cooker. Toss to coat.
3. Pour beer and vinegar over potatoes.
4. Cover and cook on **High** for 6 to 8 hours, or until potatoes are tender.
5. Stir in bacon. Spoon potato salad into serving bowl and sprinkle with parsley.

Barley Mushroom "Risotto"

I adore risotto and would eat it every day if I had the chance. This slow cooker version uses barley to produce a dish very similar to the real thing. Although this makes a hearty meatless main course, it can also be served as a side dish with beef, pork, chicken or lamb.

• • •

Tip

Pearl barley, which is the common form of barley, is the perfect grain to cook in the slow cooker. The long, slow cooking makes it tender but not gummy.

• • •

Variation

Shrimp Mushroom Risotto: Stir in $1/2$ lb (250 g) shrimp, cooked, peeled and deveined, during the final 10 minutes of cooking time.

● Slow cooker size: $3^1/2$ to 6 quart

1	package ($1/2$ oz/14 g) dried wild mushrooms, such as shiitake or chanterelles	1
1 cup	boiling water	250 mL
1 cup	pearl barley	250 mL
1	onion, finely chopped	1
$1/2$ tsp	salt	2 mL
$1/4$ tsp	freshly ground black pepper	1 mL
2 cups	vegetable stock	500 mL
$1/4$ cup	dry white wine	50 mL
$1/2$ cup	freshly grated Parmesan cheese	125 mL
$1/4$ cup	pine nuts, toasted	50 mL

1. Place mushrooms in a small bowl and pour boiling water over top. Let stand for 15 minutes, or until softened. Strain, reserving liquid. Finely chop mushrooms.

2. In slow cooker stoneware, combine barley, onion, salt, pepper, stock, wine, chopped mushrooms and reserved mushroom liquid.

3. Cover and cook on **Low** for 4 to 6 hours, or until barley is tender and liquid has been absorbed.

4. Just before serving, stir in Parmesan cheese and pine nuts.

Pine Nuts

Pine nuts are the sweet edible seeds of pine trees that are grown in places such as the southwestern United States, Italy and Mexico. To toast them, spread on a baking sheet and toast in a 350°F (160°C) oven for about 10 minutes, or until golden brown.

Middle Eastern Pilaf

Fragrant with cinnamon and spices and filled with colorful vegetables, this may be one of the best vegetarian dishes I have ever tasted.

• • •

Tips

Lentils come in a variety of colors. Try to use green or brown lentils in this dish; the smaller red lentils will break down during cooking.

When preparing the ingredients, be sure to grate the orange zest before you squeeze out the juice.

Make Ahead

Cook rice and toast almonds the day before so you can quickly stir them into the finished dish. The rest of the dish can be assembled up to 24 hours before cooking. Refrigerate overnight in slow cooker stoneware. The next day, place stoneware in slow cooker and continue to cook as directed.

● **Slow cooker size: 3 ½ to 6 quart**

1 tbsp	butter	15 mL
1	onion, finely chopped	1
2	cloves garlic, minced	2
¼ tsp	hot pepper flakes	1 mL
¼ tsp	ground cinnamon	1 mL
¼ tsp	ground coriander	1 mL
Pinch	ground allspice or cloves	Pinch
1	can (19 oz/540 mL) brown lentils, drained and rinsed	1
2	carrots, shredded or finely chopped	2
½ cup	vegetable stock or water	125 mL
½ cup	orange juice	125 mL
½ tsp	salt	2 mL
2 cups	cooked rice (about ⅔ cup/150 mL uncooked)	500 mL
2 cups	baby spinach, trimmed	500 mL
½ tsp	grated orange zest	2 mL
1 tbsp	freshly squeezed lemon juice	15 mL
¼ cup	slivered almonds, toasted (see tip, page 330)	50 mL
¼ cup	currants (optional)	50 mL

1. In a large nonstick skillet, heat butter over medium-high heat. Cook onion and garlic, stirring occasionally, for 5 minutes, or until softened. Add hot pepper flakes, cinnamon, coriander and allspice. Cook, stirring, for 1 minute, or until fragrant.

2. Transfer onion mixture to slow cooker stoneware. Add lentils, carrots, stock, orange juice and salt. Stir to combine.

3. Cover and cook on **Low** for 6 to 8 hours or on **High** for 3 to 4 hours, until hot and bubbling.

4. Add rice, spinach, orange zest, lemon juice, almonds and currants, if using. Stir to combine. Cover and cook on **High** for 10 to 15 minutes longer, or until heated through and spinach has wilted.

Pecan Mushroom Wild Rice

Buttery nuts, onions and mushrooms married with wild rice make this a noble companion for prime rib, roast chicken or baked salmon.

• • •

Tips

For added color, toss in chopped red bell pepper 15 to 20 minutes before serving time.

● Slow cooker size: 3½ to 5 quart

2 tbsp	butter or margarine	25 mL
1	onion, finely chopped	1
8 oz	sliced mushrooms	250 g
½ cup	chopped pecans or almonds	125 mL
1 cup	wild rice	250 mL
2 cups	chicken stock	500 mL

1. In a large skillet, melt butter over medium-high heat. Add onion, mushrooms and pecans; sauté for 7 to 8 minutes, or until vegetables are tender and nuts are fragrant. Add rice and cook for 3 minutes. Transfer mixture to slow cooker stoneware and pour in stock.

2. Cover and cook on **Low** for 6 to 8 hours or on **High** for 2 to 3 hours, until most of the liquid has been absorbed. Fluff with a fork before serving.

Wild Rice

Wild rice isn't actually a rice at all, but a type of grass seed that grows throughout North America. Native Americans presented it to early fur traders, and it has been prized ever since. When preparing wild rice, make sure that it is well rinsed and keep in mind that it expands to four times its uncooked volume. Add salt after cooking to ensure the proper grain expansion and to enhance the nutty flavor.

Country-Style Sage and Bread Stuffing

*Is it stuffing or dressing?
Technically, it's stuffing
when it's baked inside the
bird and dressing when it's
not. Whichever the case,
stuffing cooked inside the
slow cooker is moist,
delicious and a lot easier
to get out!*

• • •

Variations

Dried Fruit Stuffing: Add
1 cup (250 mL) chopped
dried fruit such as
cranberries, apples, raisins
and currants to stuffing
and stir in for last hour
of cooking.

Mushroom Stuffing: In a
large skillet, melt ¼ cup
(50 mL) butter over
medium heat. Add 1½ lbs
(750 g) sliced mushrooms
and cook, stirring often, for
10 to 12 minutes, or until
liquid has evaporated and
mushrooms are beginning
to brown. Stir cooked
mushrooms into stuffing
for last hour of cooking.

● **Slow cooker size: 3½ to 6 quart**

½ cup	butter	125 mL
2	onions, finely chopped	2
2	stalks celery, finely chopped	2
½ cup	finely chopped fresh parsley	125 mL
1½ tsp	dried rosemary, crumbled	7 mL
1½ tsp	dried thyme	7 mL
1½ tsp	dried marjoram	7 mL
1½ tsp	dried sage	7 mL
1½ tsp	salt	7 mL
½ tsp	ground nutmeg	2 mL
½ tsp	freshly ground black pepper	2 mL
1	loaf day-old sourdough bread, cut into ½-inch (1 cm) cubes (about 10 cups/2.5 L)	1
1½ cups	chicken, turkey or vegetable stock	375 mL

1. In a large nonstick skillet, heat butter over medium-high heat. Add onions and celery and cook, stirring occasionally, for about 10 minutes, or until onions are softened. Add parsley, rosemary, thyme, marjoram, sage, salt, nutmeg and pepper. Cook, stirring, for 1 minute.

2. Place bread cubes in a large bowl and add onion mixture; stir to combine. Slowly add stock, tossing gently to moisten. Transfer to slow cooker stoneware.

3. Cover and cook on **High** for 1 hour. Reduce heat to **Low** and cook for 2 to 3 hours longer, or until heated through. (The slow cooker will keep the stuffing at serving temperature. Keep on **Low** for up to 3 hours after stuffing is cooked.)

Wild Rice Stuffing with Almonds and Cranberries

This is a delicious special-occasion accompaniment to any roast, especially roast pork.

• • •

Tips

Wild rice is not actually rice but a long-grain marsh grass native to the northern Great Lakes region. It has a wonderful nutty flavor and chewy texture that enhance stuffings, casseroles, soups and salads.

To toast almonds: Spread on a baking sheet and bake in a 350°F (180°C) oven for 5 to 7 minutes, or until golden brown and fragrant.

● **Slow cooker size: 3½ to 6 quart**

½ cup	butter	125 mL
1	large onion, finely chopped	1
2	cloves garlic, minced	2
¼ cup	chopped fresh parsley	50 mL
1 tbsp	chopped fresh thyme (or 1 tsp/5 mL dried)	15 mL
3 cups	chicken or vegetable stock	750 mL
1 cup	uncooked wild rice	250 mL
1 cup	cooked rice (about ¼ cup/50 mL uncooked)	250 mL
½ cup	dried cranberries	125 mL
½ cup	chopped almonds, toasted (see tip, at left)	125 mL
½ cup	chopped green onions	125 mL
	Salt and freshly ground black pepper	

1. In a large nonstick skillet, melt butter over medium-high heat. Add onion and garlic and cook, stirring occasionally, for 4 to 5 minutes, or until softened. Add parsley and thyme. Cook, stirring, for 1 minute.
2. Transfer onion mixture to slow cooker stoneware. Stir in stock and wild rice.
3. Cover and cook on **Low** for 6 to 8 hours or on **High** for 3 to 4 hours, until most of liquid has been absorbed and wild rice fluffs easily with a fork.
4. Add cooked rice, cranberries, almonds and green onions; stir to combine. Cover and cook on **High** for 20 to 30 minutes longer, or until heated through. Season with salt and pepper.

Rhubarb Apple Sauce

**Makes about
2½ cups (625 mL)**

*A sure sign of spring is the
popping up of tender pink
rhubarb shoots. Make this
tangy-sweet sauce
to serve over grilled chicken
or pork or alongside a roast.*

• • •

Tip

The sauce will keep
in the refrigerator for up to
1 week or in the freezer for
up to 3 months.

● Slow cooker size: 3½ to 4 quart

2 cups	chopped fresh or frozen rhubarb (thawed if frozen)	500 mL
1 cup	unsweetened applesauce	250 mL
2 tbsp	cider vinegar	25 mL
¼ cup	packed brown sugar	50 mL
¼ cup	granulated sugar	50 mL
½ tsp	ground cinnamon	2 mL

1. In slow cooker stoneware, combine rhubarb, applesauce, vinegar, brown sugar, granulated sugar and cinnamon.
2. Cover and cook on **Low** for 3 to 4 hours or on **High** for 1 to 2 hours, until tender.

Sweet Endings

Old-Fashioned Gingerbread with Lemon Sauce

Slow-cooking this delicious cake results in a moist, heavenly scented treat just like Grandma used to make.

• • •

Tips

If you are pressed for time, you can eliminate the lemon sauce and serve the cake dusted with sifted confectioner's (icing) sugar. Applesauce also makes a wonderful accompaniment.

To get the most juice from a lemon, leave at room temperature and roll on counter, pressing down with the palm of your hand, before squeezing.

• Slow cooker size: 3½ to 6 quart

Gingerbread

½ cup	butter, softened	125 mL
½ cup	granulated sugar	125 mL
1	egg, lightly beaten	1
1 cup	fancy molasses	250 mL
2½ cups	all-purpose flour	625 mL
1½ tsp	baking soda	7 mL
2 tsp	ground ginger	10 mL
1 tsp	ground cinnamon	5 mL
½ tsp	ground cloves	2 mL
½ tsp	salt	2 mL
1 cup	hot strong coffee	250 mL

Lemon Sauce

½ cup	confectioner's (icing) sugar	125 mL
2 tsp	cornstarch	10 mL
Pinch	salt	Pinch
	Juice of 2 lemons	
½ cup	water	125 mL
1 tbsp	butter	15 mL

1. *Gingerbread:* In a large bowl, with an electric mixer, cream butter and granulated sugar. Add egg and beat for about 1 minute, or until light and fluffy. Beat in molasses.

2. In a separate bowl, sift together flour, baking soda, ginger, cinnamon, cloves and salt.

3. Stir flour mixture into butter mixture alternately with coffee, making 3 additions of flour and 2 of coffee, and mixing well after each addition.

4. Lightly grease slow cooker stoneware and line bottom with parchment paper or waxed paper cut to fit. Preheat slow cooker on **High** for 10 minutes to warm stoneware.

5. Pour batter into slow cooker. To prevent moisture from dripping onto cake batter, place two clean tea towels (folded in half to make four layers) across top of stoneware before covering with lid. Towels will absorb any moisture that accumulates during cooking.

6. Cover and cook on **Low** for 3 to 4 hours or on **High** for 1¾ to 2 hours, until a tester inserted in center of cake comes out clean. Turn out onto baking rack and remove parchment paper. Let cool slightly.

7. *Lemon sauce:* In a small saucepan, combine confectioner's sugar, cornstarch and salt.

8. Add lemon juice a little at a time, stirring to form a smooth paste. Add water; cook, stirring, over medium-high heat for about 1 minute, or until mixture thickens and bubbles. Remove from heat and stir in butter until melted.

9. Cut cake into wedges and spoon sauce over cake.

Tip

To grease slow cooker stoneware, use a vegetable nonstick spray. Or use cake pan grease, which is available in specialty cake-decorating or bulk-food stores.

Pineapple Upside-Down Cake

Serves 6 to 8

This old-time favorite uses fresh pineapple (widely available in grocery stores) spiked with ginger, pecans and orange zest. Serve with a dollop of whipped cream.

• • •

Tip

Traditionally, buttermilk was the liquid left after the butter was churned. Today, it is made commercially by adding special bacteria to give it a slightly thickened texture and tangy flavor.

● Slow cooker size: 5 to 6 quart

Fruit

2 tbsp	butter, melted	25 mL
⅔ cup	packed brown sugar	150 mL
½	pineapple, peeled and cut into about 10 slices (or one 19-oz/540 mL can sliced pineapple, drained)	½
½ cup	chopped pecans	125 mL

Cake

1 cup	all-purpose flour	250 mL
1 tsp	baking powder	5 mL
1 tsp	baking soda	5 mL
¼ tsp	salt	1 mL
¼ cup	butter, softened	50 mL
1 cup	granulated sugar	250 mL
1	egg, lightly beaten	1
1 tbsp	freshly squeezed lemon juice	15 mL
1 tsp	vanilla	5 mL
½ cup	buttermilk or sour milk	125 mL
1 tbsp	grated orange zest	15 mL

1. *Fruit:* In a small bowl, combine melted butter and brown sugar. Spread evenly over bottom of slow cooker stoneware. Arrange pineapple slices over sugar mixture. Sprinkle with pecans.

2. *Cake:* In a bowl, sift together flour, baking powder, baking soda and salt.

3. In a large bowl, cream together butter and granulated sugar until light and fluffy. Beat in egg.

4. In a small bowl or measuring cup, combine lemon juice, vanilla and buttermilk.

5. Add flour and buttermilk mixtures alternately to butter mixture, making 3 additions of flour and 2 of buttermilk, and beating well after each addition. Blend in orange zest. Spread batter over pineapple slices.

6. To prevent moisture from dripping onto cake batter, place two clean tea towels (folded in half to make four layers) across top of stoneware before covering with lid. Towels will absorb any moisture that accumulates during cooking.

7. Cover and cook on **High** for 3 to 4 hours, or until a tester inserted in center of cake comes out clean. Allow cake to cool in slow cooker. Invert onto serving plate before slicing.

Tip

"Homemade" sour milk can be used to replace a small amount of buttermilk. To sour milk, stir 1 tbsp (15 mL) cider vinegar into 1 cup (250 mL) milk. Let stand for 10 to 15 minutes to let the flavor develop.

Basic-But-Beautiful Slow Cooker Cheesecake

Serves 8 to 10

You won't believe how perfectly a cheesecake turns out when you cook it in the slow cooker — smooth and creamy, without a single crack. Make sure your pan will fit in the slow cooker before you begin to make this recipe.

• • •

Tip

If you are short of time, serve this with a store-bought fruit topping or fresh berries.

Make Ahead

This cake is best made a day ahead and allowed to chill in the refrigerator overnight. You can also freeze the cake for up to 2 weeks.

● Slow cooker size: 5 to 7 quart

Crust

¾ cup	vanilla wafer crumbs (about 15 wafers)	175 mL
2 tbsp	granulated sugar	25 mL
3 tbsp	butter, melted	45 mL

Cheesecake

2	packages (each 8 oz/250 g) cream cheese, softened	2
½ cup	granulated sugar	125 mL
¼ cup	sour cream	50 mL
2	eggs, lightly beaten	2
1 tsp	vanilla	5 mL

Fruit Topping

1	package (10 oz/300 g) frozen raspberries, strawberries or blueberries, thawed	1
⅓ cup	granulated sugar	75 mL
2 tbsp	cornstarch	25 mL
1 tbsp	freshly squeezed lemon juice	15 mL

1. *Crust:* In a bowl, combine wafer crumbs, sugar and melted butter. Mix well and press into a well-greased 7- or 8-inch (18 or 20 cm) springform pan. Freeze until ready to use.

2. *Cheesecake:* In a large bowl or food processor, combine cream cheese, sugar and sour cream. Process or beat with an electric mixer until smooth. Beat in eggs one at a time, mixing well after each addition. Beat in vanilla. Pour cheesecake mixture into prepared crust. Wrap entire pan tightly with foil and secure foil with an elastic band or string.

3. Cut a 2-foot (60 cm) length of foil in half lengthwise. Fold each strip in half lengthwise, forming two long strips. Crisscross the strips in the bottom of the slow cooker, bringing the ends of the foil strips up and clear of the stoneware rim.

4. Place springform pan in foil-lined slow cooker stoneware and pour in enough boiling water to come 1 inch (2.5 cm) up sides of pan. (If your pan fits snugly in slow cooker, add water before inserting pan.) Tuck foil ends under lid.

5. Cover and cook on **High** for 3 to 4 hours, or until edges are set and center is just slightly jiggly. Remove lid and grasp ends of foil strips to lift out cheesecake. Chill thoroughly, preferably overnight, before serving.

6. *Fruit topping:* Drain berries and reserve juice. In a small saucepan, combine sugar and cornstarch. Stir in lemon juice and reserved berry juice. Bring to a boil over medium heat and simmer, stirring, for 1 minute. Remove from heat and stir in thawed fruit. Chill. Just before serving, spread topping over cheesecake.

Variation

Mocha Marble Cheesecake: Substitute chocolate wafer crumbs for vanilla wafers and omit sugar in crust. After preparing batter, set aside 1 cup (250 mL) batter mixture. Dissolve 2 tsp (10 mL) instant coffee granules in 1 tbsp (15 mL) hot water. Fold 6 oz (175 g) melted and cooled semisweet chocolate into remaining batter along with coffee. Spread all but ½ cup (125 mL) chocolate batter in prepared pan. Spread plain mixture evenly on top. Top with remaining chocolate mixture and swirl with a knife to marble. Bake as directed.

Rhubarb Blueberry Pudding Cake

Stewed blueberries and rhubarb topped with a steamed moist cake layer make a wonderful old-fashioned dessert. I like to make this with the rhubarb from my garden. I freeze it and bring out as much as I need so it's ready at hand for special recipes such as this one.

• • •

Tip

If fresh rhubarb or blueberries are unavailable, use frozen. There is no need to thaw them first.

● Slow cooker size: 3½ to 5 quart

1 cup	chopped fresh or frozen rhubarb	250 mL
2 cups	fresh or frozen blueberries	500 mL
¼ cup	butter	50 mL
1¼ cups	granulated sugar, divided	300 mL
¾ cup	all-purpose flour	75 mL
1 tsp	baking powder	5 mL
½ tsp	ground cinnamon	2 mL
¼ tsp	ground nutmeg	1 mL
Pinch	salt	Pinch
½ cup	milk	125 mL
1 tbsp	cornstarch	15 mL
1 tsp	grated orange zest	5 mL
½ cup	freshly squeezed orange juice	125 mL
	Whipped cream (optional)	

1. Place rhubarb and blueberries in lightly greased slow cooker stoneware.
2. In a bowl, cream together butter and ¾ cup (175 mL) of the granulated sugar.
3. In another bowl, combine flour, baking powder, cinnamon, nutmeg and salt. Add to butter mixture alternately with milk. Spread over fruit in slow cooker.
4. In a small saucepan, combine cornstarch, remaining ½ cup (125 mL) granulated sugar and orange zest. Stir in orange juice. Bring to a boil over medium-high heat; cook, stirring constantly, until slightly thickened. Remove from heat and pour over batter in slow cooker.
5. Cover and cook on **High** for 2 to 3 hours, or until top is golden and fruit is bubbly. Serve warm with dollops of whipped cream, if desired.

Amaretti Pear Crisp

Serves 6 to 8

This is a wonderful dessert to serve in pear season. Amaretti cookies are available at most Italian delis and supermarkets. Gingersnaps are a good alternative, or you can use honey graham crackers, though they will give this dish a very different taste.

• • •

Tips

To crush cookies, process in a food processor or blender, or place in a resealable plastic bag. Squeeze all air out of bag and seal. Crush cookies with a rolling pin until crumbs are formed.

Serve the crisp warm with vanilla ice cream, Devon-style custard or whipped cream.

● **Slow cooker size: 3½ to 6 quart**

3 lbs	ripe pears (about 7 or 8)	1.5 kg
½ cup	chopped dried apricots	125 mL
¼ cup	granulated sugar	50 mL
¼ cup	amaretto liqueur, dark rum or pear nectar	50 mL

Topping

1 cup	crushed amaretti or gingersnap cookies (see tip, at left)	250 mL
½ cup	all-purpose flour	125 mL
⅓ cup	packed brown sugar	75 mL
2 tbsp	granulated sugar	25 mL
⅓ cup	cold butter, cut into cubes	75 mL

1. Peel pears, cut in half, remove cores and cut each half into 3 slices.
2. In a large bowl, combine pears, apricots, granulated sugar and Amaretto. Transfer to slow cooker stoneware.
3. *Topping:* In a separate bowl, combine crushed cookies, flour, brown sugar and granulated sugar.
4. With a pastry blender or two knives, cut in butter until mixture resembles small peas. Sprinkle over pear mixture.
5. Cover and cook on **Low** for 6 to 8 hours or on **High** for 3 to 4 hours, until tender.

Cranberry Apple Cobbler

Grab a spoon and sink into a cozy chair or sofa to enjoy this comfort-food classic. Here, tangy cranberries are paired with sweet apples under a soft, light cake topping.

• • •

Tips

Serve this cobbler warm with ice cream or drizzle with homemade or store-bought custard sauce.

When they're in season, purchase 2 or 3 extra bags of cranberries and toss them into the freezer to have on hand anytime. There is no need to defrost before using.

● **Slow cooker size: 3 ½ to 5 quart**

1	package (12 oz/340 g) cranberries, fresh or frozen	1
¾ cup	granulated sugar	175 mL
3 tbsp	cornstarch	45 mL
½ tsp	ground cinnamon	2 mL
1 cup	cranberry juice	250 mL
8 cups	sliced peeled apples (about 6)	2 L

Topping

1 ½ cups	all-purpose flour	375 mL
⅓ cup	granulated sugar	75 mL
1 tbsp	baking powder	15 mL
¼ tsp	salt	1 mL
½ cup	cold butter, cut into cubes	125 mL
⅔ cup	milk	150 mL
1 tsp	granulated sugar	5 mL
¼ tsp	ground cinnamon	1 mL

1. Place cranberries in bottom of slow cooker stoneware. Add sugar, cornstarch and cinnamon, tossing to coat. Add cranberry juice and apples; stir to combine.
2. Cover and cook on **Low** for 6 to 8 hours or on **High** for 3 to 4 hours, until apples are tender.
3. *Topping:* In a bowl, combine flour, sugar, baking powder and salt. With a pastry blender or two knives, cut in butter until mixture resembles coarse crumbs. Drizzle with milk and stir with a fork until a thick batter forms.
3. Drop batter by spoonfuls over fruit mixture. Cover and cook on **High** for 30 to 45 minutes longer, or until a toothpick inserted in the center of dumplings comes out clean.
4. In a bowl, combine sugar and cinnamon; sprinkle over dumplings before serving.

Plum Cobbler

Sweet, juicy red plums are perfect in this simple old-fashioned cobbler. Serve it with vanilla sauce (page 363) or ice cream.

• • •

Tip

You can also use peaches or pears in this recipe. Add 1 tbsp (15 mL) lemon juice to help prevent the fruit from turning brown.

● Slow cooker size: 3½ to 5 quart

7 cups	sliced pitted red plums	1.75 L
⅓ cup	packed brown sugar	75 mL
1 tbsp	cornstarch	15 mL
Pinch	ground cloves	Pinch

Topping

1½ cups	all-purpose flour	375 mL
⅓ cup	granulated sugar	75 mL
1 tbsp	baking powder	15 mL
¼ tsp	salt	1 mL
2 tsp	grated orange zest	10 mL
½ cup	cold butter, cut into cubes	125 mL
⅔ cup	milk	150 mL
1 tsp	vanilla	5 mL

1. Place plums in slow cooker stoneware.
2. In a bowl, combine brown sugar, cornstarch and cloves. Spoon over fruit and toss to coat.
3. Cover and cook on **Low** for 6 to 8 hours or on **High** for 3 to 4 hours, until fruit is bubbling.
4. *Topping:* In a bowl, combine flour, granulated sugar, baking powder, salt and orange zest. With a pastry blender or two knives, cut in butter until mixture resembles coarse crumbs.
5. In a measuring cup or small bowl, combine milk and vanilla. Pour into flour mixture and stir with a fork until a thick batter forms.
6. Drop batter by spoonfuls over fruit mixture. Cover and cook on **High** for 30 to 45 minutes longer, or until a tester inserted in center of topping comes out clean. Serve warm.

Aunt Beatty's Betty

This wonderful dessert reminds me of the traditional one my Aunt Beatty, a charming English lady, used to make. Be sure to serve it warm with whipping cream, vanilla ice cream or Lazy Cream (see recipe, page 364).

• • •

Tip

To quickly soften butter, remove foil wrapping and place cold butter in microwave-safe dish. For every ½ cup (125 mL) butter, microwave on Defrost for 45 seconds to 1 minute.

● Slow cooker size: 3½ to 5 quart

6	large baking apples, peeled and sliced	6
2 tbsp	granulated sugar	25 mL
1 tsp	ground cinnamon	5 mL

Topping

½ cup	butter, softened	125 mL
1 cup	lightly packed brown sugar	250 mL
¾ cup	all-purpose flour	175 mL

1. In a large bowl, toss together apples, sugar and cinnamon. Transfer to slow cooker stoneware.
2. *Topping:* In a bowl, combine butter and brown sugar. Add flour and mix together with a spoon until mixture is crumbly. Sprinkle over apples and pat firmly into a crust.
3. Cover and cook on **High** for 3 to 4 hours, or until apples are tender and sauce is bubbly.

Double Berry Maple Crumble

Blueberries and blackberries are a wonderful combination in this old-fashioned crumble. If you can't find blackberries, substitute raspberries.

• • •

Tips

Fruit crisps and crumbles have a natural affinity for cream, whether it's ice cream, sour cream or whipped cream. You can cut back on the fat by serving this with frozen vanilla yogurt, light sour cream or fresh fruit yogurt instead.

If you are using frozen berries, there is no need to defrost them. As the slow cooker heats up, it will thaw and cook the fruit.

● Slow cooker size: 3 ½ to 6 quart

1 cup	all-purpose flour	250 mL
½ cup	chopped walnuts	125 mL
⅔ cup	packed brown sugar	150 mL
½ cup	cold butter, cut into cubes	125 mL
4 cups	fresh or frozen blueberries	1 L
1 cup	fresh or frozen blackberries or raspberries	250 mL
⅔ cup	maple syrup	150 mL
1 tbsp	cornstarch	15 mL
2 tbsp	freshly squeezed lemon juice	25 mL

1. In a bowl, combine flour, walnuts and brown sugar. Cut in butter using a pastry blender or two knives until well blended and mixture is the size of small peas.
2. In slow cooker stoneware, combine blueberries, blackberries, maple syrup, cornstarch and lemon juice. Toss to coat. Sprinkle flour mixture over berries.
3. Cover and cook on **Low** for 6 to 8 hours or on **High** for 3 to 4 hours, until fruit is tender and juices bubble.

Brown Sugar and Coconut Baked Apples

Come home to the wonderful smell of apples baking with butter and spices. If you wish, sprinkle the baked apples with a little toasted coconut (see tip, page 354) before serving.

• • •

Tips

If you have an odd apple that doesn't want to stand upright in the slow cooker, cut a thin slice off the bottom.

This dish is best made in a large oval slow cooker. If you have a smaller model, reduce the apples to 3 or 4 (depending on what you can fit in) and make half the filling mixture.

● Slow cooker size: 5 to 6 quart

6	baking apples, such as Cortland, Spy or McIntosh	6
2 tbsp	packed brown sugar	25 mL
2 tbsp	flaked sweetened coconut	25 mL
1 tsp	ground cinnamon	5 mL
½ tsp	ground nutmeg	2 mL
¼ cup	maple syrup	50 mL
6 tbsp	cold butter	90 mL
1 cup	apple juice	250 mL

1. Peel skin off top quarter of each apple. Using a melon baller, scoop out core, leaving bottom of apple intact. Stand apples upright in slow cooker stoneware.
2. In a bowl, combine brown sugar, coconut, cinnamon and nutmeg. Fill apple cavities with sugar mixture.
3. Spoon about 2 tsp (10 mL) maple syrup into each cavity. Place 1 tbsp (15 mL) butter on each apple. Pour apple juice around apples.
4. Cover and cook on **Low** for 6 to 8 hours or on **High** for 3 to 4 hours, until apples are tender.
5. Place apples in individual serving bowls and spoon sauce around apples.

Bananas with Honey-Roasted Nuts

Serve this with vanilla ice cream and drizzle a little banana liqueur (or your favorite liqueur) on top before serving.

• • •

Tips

Look for bananas with skins that still show a little green. They will be slightly firm to start but will soften as they cook. To stop the bananas from turning brown too quickly, rub or brush the cut sides with a little lemon juice after peeling.

Buy honey-roasted peanuts or try using Best Beer Nuts (page 63).

● Slow cooker size 3½ to 6 quart

1 cup	packed brown sugar	250 mL
⅓ cup	butter, melted	75 mL
1 tbsp	hot water	15 mL
½ tsp	vanilla	2 mL
8	bananas, just ripened, peeled and halved lengthwise	8
½ cup	chopped honey-roasted peanuts	125 mL

1. In a small bowl, combine brown sugar, melted butter, water and vanilla. Mix well.
2. Arrange bananas, cut side up, in bottom of lightly greased slow cooker stoneware. Pour sugar mixture over bananas.
3. Cover and cook on **Low** for 3 to 4 hours, or until sauce is bubbling.
4. Spoon warm bananas into serving bowls and sprinkle with chopped peanuts.

Caramel Peaches

This easy-to-make dessert combines fresh juicy peaches with a sweet butterscotch sauce. It's the perfect dish to whip together when unexpected guests arrive.

• • •

Tips

Serve these peaches over vanilla ice cream or simply enjoy them on their own. You can substitute sliced apples for the peaches.

To quickly ripen fresh peaches, place in a brown paper bag and let stand overnight at room temperature.

To peel peaches, plunge in boiling water for 30 seconds to loosen skin and quickly plunge into cold water. Skin should easily slip off.

● Slow cooker size: 3½ to 5 quart

6	peaches, peeled and sliced, or 3 cans (each 14 oz/398 mL) peach halves, drained and sliced	6
2 tsp	freshly squeezed lemon juice	10 mL
1 cup	packed brown sugar	250 mL
3 tbsp	melted butter or margarine	45 mL
¼ cup	whipping (35%) cream	50 mL
½ tsp	ground cinnamon	2 mL
	Vanilla ice cream (optional)	

1. In a bowl, toss together peach slices and lemon juice.
2. In slow cooker stoneware, combine brown sugar, butter, cream and cinnamon; mix well. Add peach slices and toss to coat with brown sugar mixture.
3. Cover and cook on **Low** for 4 to 6 hours, until fruit is bubbling.
4. If desired, serve over vanilla ice cream.

Maple-Sauced Pears

This luscious dessert is utterly simple but a real crowd pleaser. Serve it at room temperature garnished with whipped cream or a little toasted coconut (see tip, page 354).

• • •

Tips

The best pears to choose for this dessert are Bartletts, with the shapely Bosc a good alternative. Buy the pears a few days before using and allow them to ripen at room temperature until juicy but firm. Rub the pears with lemon juice to prevent them from discoloring after they have been peeled.

This recipe works best in a 3½-quart slow cooker, because the pears remain partially submerged in the sauce.

● Slow cooker size: 3½ to 6 quart

6	firm but ripe pears	6
⅓ cup	maple syrup	75 mL
¼ cup	packed brown sugar	50 mL
1 tbsp	butter, melted	15 mL
1 tsp	grated orange zest	5 mL
1 tbsp	cornstarch	15 mL
2 tbsp	water	25 mL

1. Peel pears and core them from the bottom, leaving the stems attached. Place pears upright in slow cooker stoneware.
2. In a bowl, combine maple syrup, brown sugar, melted butter and orange zest. Pour over pears.
3. Cover and cook on **High** for 2 to 3 hours, or until pears are tender. Gently remove pears from slow cooker and place in serving dishes.
4. In a small bowl or jar, combine cornstarch and water (see box, below). Stir into sauce in slow cooker. Cover and cook on **High** for 10 minutes longer, or until sauce thickens. Spoon sauce over pears.

Cornstarch

A quick way to mix cornstarch with a liquid is to use a jar. Screw the lid on tightly and shake the jar until the mixture is smooth. (This is faster than trying to stir or whisk until all the cornstarch is dissolved.)

Honey-Orange Crème Caramel

This decadent treat will remind you of the rich dessert that you get in expensive restaurants. Slow cooking ensures a smooth, creamy custard without overbaking.

• • •

Tips

You will need a large (5- to 7-quart) slow cooker so your soufflé dish or bowl will fit and can be easily removed.

Custard-type recipes work best in the slow cooker when they are baked in a soufflé dish placed in the stoneware insert. If cooked directly in the stoneware, the eggs in the custard will have a tendency to curdle during the long cooking process.

● **Slow cooker size: 5 to 7 quart**

I cup	granulated sugar	250 mL
½ cup	water	125 mL

Honey-Orange Custard

I	can (13 oz/385 mL) evaporated milk	I
¼ cup	1% or 2% milk	50 mL
I	strip orange zest	I
3	eggs, lightly beaten	3
¼ cup	liquid honey	50 mL
I tbsp	Grand Marnier or orange juice	15 mL

1. In a saucepan over medium heat, combine sugar and water. Stirring constantly with a wooden spoon, cook until sugar is dissolved and mixture comes to a boil. Stop stirring and continue to cook for 4 minutes, or until golden brown. (Alternatively, place sugar and water mixture in microwave; cover tightly with plastic wrap but leave slight space for steam to escape. Cook on High for 8 to 10 minutes or until golden brown.) Pour into 6½ cup (1.6 L) soufflé dish, tilting dish to distribute syrup evenly over bottom and up the sides. Set aside.

2. *Honey-orange custard:* In a saucepan over medium-low heat, combine evaporated milk, milk and orange zest. Gently heat until mixture begins to simmer. Remove from heat and let stand for 10 minutes. With a fork, remove zest from saucepan and discard.

3. In a bowl, combine eggs, honey and Grand Marnier. Gradually whisk in warm milk mixture. Pour into sugar-coated soufflé dish. Cover with foil and secure with an elastic band.

4. Cut a 2-foot (60 cm) length of foil in half lengthwise. Fold each strip in half lengthwise, forming two long strips. Crisscross the strips in the bottom of the slow cooker, bringing the ends of the foil strips up and clear of the stoneware rim. Place soufflé dish in slow cooker and pour in about 2 cups (500 mL) hot water. (If soufflé dish fits snugly in slow cooker, add water before placing dish in cooker.) Tuck foil ends under lid.

5. Cover and cook on **High** for 2 to 2½ hours, or until knife inserted in custard comes out clean. Remove lid and grasp ends of foil strips to lift out soufflé dish. Refrigerate for 3 to 4 hours or overnight.

6. To unmold, run a sharp knife around outside edge of custard. Dip bottom of dish in hot water for a few moments and invert onto a serving plate, giving a firm shake to release the custard and sauce.

Make Ahead
This dessert is best made ahead so it can be chilled before serving. Make it early in the day or even a full day ahead.

Collapsible Vegetable Steamers

To keep a baking dish raised off the bottom of your slow cooker, you can use a trivet or small baking rack. But I find that a collapsible vegetable steamer also works well — and it's useful for lifting the bowl out of the slow cooker. Place steamer on the bottom of stoneware and open it as much as possible. Place soufflé dish or bowl on steamer and pour in enough water to come 1 inch (2.5 cm) up sides. Steam as directed.

Baked Lemon Sponge

As this lovely old-fashioned dessert steams in the slow cooker, it separates into a cake-like topping with a creamy lemon custard sauce underneath. Sprinkle with icing sugar before serving.

• • •

Tips

You will need a large (5- to 7-quart) slow cooker so your soufflé dish or bowl will fit and can be easily removed.

To get the most juice from a lemon, leave at room temperature and roll on counter, pressing down with the palm of your hand, before squeezing.

To zest a lemon, use the fine edge of a cheese grater, ensuring you don't grate the white pith underneath. Or use a zester to remove the zest, then finely chop. Zesters are inexpensive and widely available at specialty kitchen shops.

● Slow cooker size: 5 to 7 quart

1 cup	granulated sugar	250 mL
¼ cup	all-purpose flour	50 mL
¼ tsp	salt	1 mL
1 tbsp	grated lemon zest	15 mL
¼ cup	freshly squeezed lemon juice	50 mL
3	eggs, separated	3
1 tbsp	melted butter	15 mL
1 cup	milk	250 mL
1 tbsp	icing sugar	15 mL
	Fresh raspberries and blueberries	

1. In a bowl combine sugar, flour and salt. Stir in lemon zest, lemon juice, egg yolks, butter and milk.

2. In another bowl, beat egg whites until stiff peaks form; fold gently into lemon mixture. Pour into a lightly greased 6-cup (1.5 L) soufflé dish or bowl. Cover tightly with foil and secure with an elastic band.

3. Cut a 2-foot (60 cm) length of foil in half lengthwise. Fold each strip in half lengthwise, forming two long strips. Crisscross the strips in the bottom of the slow cooker, bringing the ends of the foil strips up and clear of the stoneware rim. Place soufflé dish in slow cooker and pour in enough water to come 1 inch (2.5 cm) up sides of soufflé dish. (If soufflé dish fits snugly in slow cooker, add water before placing dish in cooker.) Tuck foil ends under lid.

4. Cover and cook on **High** for 2 to 3 hours, or until topping is set and light and fluffy. Remove lid and grasp ends of foil strips to lift out soufflé dish.

5. Sift icing sugar over sponge and serve with fresh berries.

Pumpkin Pie Custard Dessert

What's a holiday dinner without a pumpkin dessert? You will never miss the crust in this easy-to-make custard. Crisp gingersnap cookies sprinkled over the top add a tasty crunch. Serve with whipped cream.

• • •

Tip

Make sure the soufflé dish will fit in your slow cooker before you start to make the recipe.

• • •

Variation

Pumpkin Crème Brûlée:
Omit the gingersnap crumbs and refrigerate custard until well chilled (up to 2 days). Sprinkle top with $1/2$ cup (125 mL) packed brown sugar and broil 6 inches (15 cm) from heat for 2 to 6 minutes, or until sugar bubbles and darkens. Chill, uncovered, for at least 30 minutes or up to 3 hours before serving.

● **Slow cooker size: 5 to 6 quart**

1	can (19 oz/540 mL) pumpkin pie filling	1
1	can (13 oz/385 mL) evaporated milk	1
2	eggs, lightly beaten	2
1 cup	gingersnap cookie crumbs (see tip, page 341)	250 mL

1. In a bowl, whisk together pie filling, evaporated milk and eggs. Pour into an ungreased 4-cup (1 L) soufflé dish. Cover entire dish tightly with foil and secure foil with string or elastic band.

2. Cut a 2-foot (60 cm) length of foil in half lengthwise. Fold each strip in half lengthwise, forming two long strips. Crisscross the strips in the bottom of the slow cooker, bringing the ends of the foil strips up and clear of the stoneware rim. Place soufflé dish in slow cooker and pour in enough boiling water to come 1 inch (2.5 cm) up sides of soufflé dish. (If soufflé dish fits snugly in slow cooker, add water before placing dish in cooker.) Tuck foil ends under lid.

3. Cover and cook on **High** for $3 1/2$ to 4 hours, or until a tester inserted in center of custard comes out clean. Remove lid and grasp ends of foil strips to lift out soufflé dish. Transfer to a wire rack.

4. Serve warm with gingersnap crumbs sprinkled on top.

Almond-Pear Steamed Pudding with Coconut-Lime Sauce

Serves 6 to 8		

This lovely steamed pudding combines two of my favorite ingredients — pears and toasted coconut.

• • •

Tips

For the purée, use canned pears or two very ripe, fresh pears — or use a small jar of baby food pears, which is just the right size for the amount suggested in this recipe.

If you like a smooth, clear sauce, omit the coconut. However, I love the texture it adds.

To toast coconut: Spread onto a baking sheet and bake in a 350°F (180°C) oven, stirring once or twice, for 7 to 8 minutes, or until golden brown. Remove from heat and let cool completely.

● **Slow cooker size: 5 to 7 quart**

¼ cup	butter, softened	50 mL
3 tbsp	almond paste or marzipan, softened	45 mL
¾ cup	granulated sugar, divided	175 mL
I cup	cake and pastry flour	250 mL
I tsp	baking powder	5 mL
½ cup	shredded sweetened coconut, toasted	125 mL
2	whole eggs	2
½ tsp	almond extract	2 mL
½ cup	puréed pears, canned or fresh (see tip, at left)	125 mL
I	egg white	I

Coconut-Lime Sauce

¾ cup	granulated sugar	175 mL
2 tbsp	cornstarch	25 mL
I cup	water	250 mL
I tsp	grated lime zest	5 mL
¼ cup	freshly squeezed lime juice	50 mL
½ cup	shredded sweetened coconut, toasted	125 mL

1. In a large bowl, beat together butter, almond paste and ½ cup (125 mL) sugar until light and fluffy.

2. In a separate bowl, sift together flour and baking powder. Stir in coconut. Add eggs, almond extract and pears, mixing until smooth. Gradually stir in almond paste mixture.

3. In a small bowl, beat egg white until foamy; add remaining 2 tbsp (25 mL) sugar and beat until soft peaks form. Gently fold egg white into batter and pour batter into a lightly greased 6-cup (1.5 L) pudding mold or heavy bowl. Secure cover on pudding mold, or cover bowl with aluminum foil and secure with an elastic band.

4. Cut a 2-foot (60 cm) length of foil in half lengthwise. Fold each strip in half lengthwise, forming two long strips. Crisscross the strips in the bottom of the slow cooker, bringing the ends of the foil strips up and clear of the stoneware rim. Place pudding mold in slow cooker and pour in enough boiling water to come 1 inch (2.5 cm) up sides of mold. (If pudding mold fits snugly in slow cooker, add water before placing mold in cooker.) Tuck foil ends under lid.

5. Cover and cook on **High** for 4 to 5 hours (do not cook for a longer time on **Low**), or until a tester inserted in center of pudding comes out clean. (Pudding will look moist around the edges.) Remove lid and grasp ends of foil strips to lift out pudding mold. Let cool for 5 minutes.

6. To unmold, run a knife around edges of pudding to loosen. Invert onto a serving platter and carefully lift off mold. Let cool to room temperature.

7. *Coconut-lime sauce:* In a saucepan over medium-high heat, combine sugar and cornstarch. Whisk in water and lime juice. Cook, stirring constantly, until mixture comes to a boil. Reduce heat and simmer, stirring constantly, until thickened. Stir in coconut and lime zest. Serve sauce over pudding.

Tip

You will need a large (5- to 7-quart) slow cooker so your soufflé dish or bowl will fit and can be easily removed.

Steamed Cranberry Pudding with Grand Marnier Sauce

This cranberry-dotted pudding comes from Carol Ferguson and Canadian Living *magazine. It's a pleasant alternative to traditional holiday plum pudding, although it can be enjoyed at any time of the year.*

• • •

Tips

You will need a large (5- to 7-quart) slow cooker so your pudding mold or bowl will fit and can be easily removed. Be sure to use long oven mitts when lifting out the mold so the steam doesn't burn your arms.

If you have an old-fashioned pudding bowl with a lid, it will be ideal for this recipe. But a 6-cup (1.5 L) heavy glass mixing bowl will work equally well.

● Slow cooker size: 5 to 7 quart

1 cup	chopped cranberries, fresh or frozen (not thawed)	250 mL
¾ cup	granulated sugar, divided	175 mL
½ cup	butter, softened	125 mL
2	eggs	2
1½ cups	all-purpose flour	375 mL
1½ tsp	baking powder	7 mL
Pinch	salt	Pinch
2 tbsp	milk	25 mL
1 tbsp	grated orange zest	15 mL

Grand Marnier Sauce

½ cup	packed brown sugar	125 mL
2 tbsp	cornstarch	25 mL
¼ tsp	salt	1 mL
1½ cups	water	375 mL
2 tbsp	butter	25 mL
3 tbsp	Grand Marnier or any orange liqueur or orange juice concentrate	45 mL

1. In a bowl, toss together cranberries and ¼ cup (50 mL) of the granulated sugar. Set aside.
2. In a bowl, with an electric mixer, cream butter. Add remaining ½ cup (125 mL) granulated sugar and beat until light and fluffy. Beat in eggs, one at a time.
3. In another bowl, stir together flour, baking powder and salt. Add to butter mixture, a little at a time, alternately with milk. (Mixture will be very thick.) Stir in orange zest. Spoon into a lightly greased 6-cup (1.5 L) pudding mold or heavy bowl. Cover with lid or foil and secure with elastic band.

4. Cut a 2-foot (60 cm) length of foil in half lengthwise. Fold each strip in half lengthwise, forming two long strips. Crisscross the strips in the bottom of the slow cooker, bringing the ends of the foil strips up and clear of the stoneware rim. Place pudding mold in slow cooker and pour in enough boiling water to come 1 inch (2.5 cm) up sides of mold. (If pudding mold fits snugly in slow cooker, add water before placing mold in cooker.) Tuck foil ends under lid.

5. Cover and cook on **High** for 4½ to 5 hours (do not cook for a longer time on **Low**), or until a tester inserted in center of pudding comes out clean. (Pudding will look slightly moist around the edges.) Remove lid and grasp ends of foil strips to lift out pudding mold. Let cool for 10 minutes, then turn out onto a serving plate.

6. *Grand Marnier sauce:* In a saucepan, over medium-high heat, combine brown sugar, cornstarch and salt. Stir in water and bring mixture to a boil. Reduce heat to medium and cook, whisking constantly, for 3 minutes, or until thickened. Stir in butter and Grand Marnier, adding more liqueur if desired. Serve sauce spooned over pudding or in a sauce boat to pass at the table.

Tip

When they're in season, purchase 2 or 3 extra bags of cranberries and toss them into the freezer to have on hand anytime. There is no need to defrost before using.

Carrot Marmalade Pudding with Lemon Sauce

Serves 4

Instead of a traditional Christmas pudding, my mother makes a carrot pudding. It's every bit as satisfying — and every bit as spectacular to watch when doused with brandy and set aflame. I love it with the citrusy lemon sauce featured here, but feel free to try it with the caramel sauce on page 360.

• • •

Tips

You will need a large (5- to 7-quart) slow cooker so your pudding mold or bowl will fit and can be easily removed. Be sure to use long oven mitts when lifting out the bowl so the steam doesn't burn your arms.

If you don't have a pudding mold, a heat-proof mixing bowl works very well. Instead of a lid, use aluminum foil secured with an elastic band.

● Slow cooker size: 5 to 7 quart

1 1/4 cups	grated carrots	300 mL
1 cup	fine dry bread crumbs	250 mL
1 cup	packed brown sugar	250 mL
1/2 cup	chopped dates	125 mL
1/2 cup	chopped candied cherries	125 mL
1/2 cup	chopped walnuts or pecans	125 mL
1/2 cup	seedless raisins	125 mL
1/2 cup	golden raisins or currants	125 mL
1/2 cup	shortening, softened	125 mL
1/4 cup	butter, softened	50 mL
3	eggs, lightly beaten	3
1/4 cup	orange marmalade	50 mL
2 tbsp	molasses	25 mL
2 tbsp	dry sherry or white grape juice	25 mL
1 cup	all-purpose flour	250 mL
1 tsp	baking powder	5 mL
1/2 tsp	baking soda	2mL
1 tsp	salt	5 mL
1 tsp	ground cinnamon	5 mL
1/2 tsp	ground nutmeg	2 mL
1/2 tsp	ground allspice	2 mL
1/4 tsp	ground cloves	1 mL

Lemon Sauce

1/2 cup	granulated sugar	125 mL
1 tbsp	cornstarch	15 mL
1 cup	boiling water	250 mL
2 tbsp	butter	25 mL
1/2 tsp	grated lemon zest	2 mL
2 tbsp	freshly squeezed lemon juice	25 mL

1. In a bowl, combine carrots, bread crumbs, brown sugar, dates, cherries, walnuts, seedless raisins and golden raisins; stir to mix well and set aside.

2. In a separate bowl, beat shortening and butter together until light and fluffy. Add eggs, one at a time, beating well after each addition. Add marmalade, molasses and sherry; mix well.

3. In a separate bowl, sift together flour, baking powder, baking soda, salt, cinnamon, nutmeg, allspice and cloves; beat into shortening mixture to form a batter. Fold fruit into batter, stirring until just combined.

4. Pour batter into a lightly greased 6-cup (1.5 L) pudding mold or bowl. Cover with lid or foil and secure with elastic band.

5. Cut a 2-foot (60 cm) length of foil in half lengthwise. Fold each strip in half lengthwise, forming two long strips. Crisscross the strips in the bottom of the slow cooker, bringing the ends of the foil strips up and clear of the stoneware rim. Place pudding mold in slow cooker and pour in enough boiling water to come 1 inch (2.5 cm) up sides of mold. (If pudding mold fits snugly in slow cooker, add water before placing mold in cooker.) Tuck foil ends under lid.

6. Cover and cook on **High** for 4½ to 5 hours (do not cook for a longer time on **Low**), or until a tester inserted in center of pudding comes out clean. Remove lid and grasp ends of foil strips to lift out pudding mold. Let cool for 5 minutes.

7. To unmold, run a knife around edges of pudding to loosen. Invert onto a serving platter and carefully lift off mold. Set aside to cool.

8. *Lemon sauce:* In a saucepan over low heat, mix together granulated sugar and cornstarch. Whisk in boiling water. Cook over medium heat until thickened and clear, stirring frequently. Remove from heat and stir in butter, lemon zest and lemon juice. Serve warm over pudding.

Tip

To grate lemon or orange zest, a zester tool can be purchased very inexpensively at kitchen shops. Or you can use the smallest holes on a cheese grater.

Apricot Croissant Pudding with Caramel Sauce

Serves 10 to 12

Croissants and orange liqueur make this bread pudding super-decadent. If you are short of time, use a store-bought caramel sauce.

• • •

Tips

Evaporated milk holds up extremely well in slow cookers and will not curdle. Don't confuse this milk with the sweetened condensed milk used in desserts and candies.

You'll need about 12 large croissants, or buy twice as many mini croissants, which chop up nicely. Many supermarkets now carry the frozen variety, which need to be baked first.

• Slow cooker size: 5 to 6 quart

3	cans (each 13 oz/385 mL) evaporated milk	3
6	eggs, lightly beaten	6
½ cup	granulated sugar	125 mL
¼ cup	Grand Marnier or orange juice	50 mL
½ tsp	ground nutmeg	2 mL
12 cups	chopped croissants	3 L
1 cup	chopped dried apricots	250 mL

Caramel Sauce

1 cup	granulated sugar	250 mL
2 tbsp	water	25 mL
2 tbsp	corn syrup	25 mL
½ cup	whipping (35%) cream	125 mL
¼ cup	butter	50 mL
½ tsp	vanilla	2 mL

1. In a large bowl, whisk together evaporated milk, eggs, sugar, Grand Marnier and nutmeg until smooth (or combine in a blender).

2. Place croissant pieces in lightly greased slow cooker stoneware. Add apricots and toss to combine.

3. Pour custard over croissant-apricot mixture, pressing down gently with a spatula so croissants and apricots are evenly covered. Let stand for 20 minutes.

4. Cover and cook on **High** for 3 to 4 hours, or until pudding is golden brown on top and firm to the touch. (If sides begin to burn, reduce heat to **Low** and continue as directed.) Cool slightly.

5. *Caramel sauce:* In a saucepan, combine sugar, water and corn syrup over medium-low heat until sugar dissolves. Increase heat to medium-high. Boil without stirring for about 8 minutes, or until syrup turns amber. Brush down sides of pan with a wet pastry brush and swirl pan occasionally.

6. Remove sauce from heat. Whisk in whipping cream, butter and vanilla (mixture will bubble vigorously).

7. Place pan over low heat and cook, stirring, for about 2 minutes, or until sauce thickens slightly.

8. Spoon pudding into individual bowls and drizzle with caramel sauce.

Make Ahead

The caramel sauce can be prepared a day ahead. Cover and chill. Rewarm in a saucepan over medium-low heat before serving.

Upside-Down Fudge Brownie Pudding

Serves 4 to 6

In this wonderfully rich dessert, the fudgy batter rises to the top, leaving a delicious chocolate sauce beneath.

• • •

Tips

Vanilla ice cream is a must with this dish! If you happen to have any left over, refrigerate and eat cold the next day. It's equally delicious.

To grease slow cooker stoneware, use a vegetable nonstick spray. Or use cake pan grease, which is available in specialty cake-decorating or bulk-food stores.

● **Slow cooker size: 3½ to 5 quart**

1 cup	all-purpose flour	250 mL
2 tsp	baking powder	10 mL
¾ cup	granulated sugar	175 mL
5 tbsp	unsweetened cocoa powder, divided	75 mL
½ cup	milk	125 mL
2 tbsp	butter, melted	25 mL
1 tsp	vanilla	5 mL
¼ cup	chopped walnuts (optional)	50 mL
¾ cup	packed brown sugar	175 mL
2 cups	boiling water	500 mL
	Vanilla ice cream	

1. In a bowl, combine flour, baking powder, sugar and 3 tbsp (45 mL) of the cocoa; mix well.

2. In another bowl, combine milk, butter and vanilla. Stir into flour mixture with walnuts. The batter will be very thick. Spread evenly in lightly greased slow cooker stoneware.

3. In a bowl, combine brown sugar and remaining 2 tbsp (25 mL) cocoa. Add boiling water, mixing well. Pour over batter in slow cooker.

4. Cover and cook on **High** for 2 hours, or until a toothpick inserted in the center of the pudding comes out clean.

5. Spoon into individual bowls and serve with scoops of vanilla ice cream.

Double Chocolate Caramel Bread Pudding

Serves 8 to 10

When you are in the mood to splurge, this dessert fits the bill. To guild the lily, serve it with the easy vanilla sauce.

• • •

Tip

For added extravagance, try using chocolate bread. It can be found at specialty bakeries or by special request at the supermarket bakery.

Make Ahead

This dish can be completely assembled and refrigerated up to 24 hours before serving. The next day, place stoneware in slow cooker and continue to cook as directed.

● **Slow cooker size: 3½ to 6 quart**

6	thick slices white or egg bread, crusts removed, cut into 1-inch (2.5 cm) cubes (about 6 cups/1.5 L)	6
1 cup	white chocolate chips	250 mL
2½ cups	hot milk	625 mL
1 cup	packed brown sugar	250 mL
3	eggs, lightly beaten	3
2 tbsp	butter, melted	25 mL
1 tsp	vanilla	5 mL
3	chocolate caramel bars or rolls (2 oz/52 g) , broken into sections	3

Vanilla Sauce (optional)

1 cup	premium vanilla ice cream, melted	250 mL
2 tbsp	amaretto liqueur	25 mL

1. Place bread cubes in lightly greased slow cooker stoneware.
2. Place white chocolate chips in a bowl. Pour in hot milk and let rest for 5 minutes. Whisk until smooth.
3. In a large bowl, whisk together brown sugar, eggs, melted butter and vanilla. Beat in white chocolate mixture and pour over bread cubes. Press pieces of chocolate caramel bar evenly into bread. Let stand for 20 minutes.
4. Cover and cook on **High** for 3 to 4 hours, or until a tester inserted in center comes out clean.
5. *Vanilla sauce (if using):* Stir together vanilla ice cream and liqueur until smooth.
6. To serve, spoon warm bread pudding into individual serving dishes and spoon sauce over pudding.

Bayou Bread Pudding with Rum Sauce and Lazy Cream

I was inspired to make this dish after our book club read a wonderful tale set in the steamy heart of the Bayou. This dessert is so-o-o-o-o authentically good, everyone will be saying "y'all" by the end of the evening.

● ● ●

Tip

To make the bread cubes: Cut the bread into ½-inch (1 cm) slices, then cut each slice into 4 pieces. If you have the time, cut bread into cubes the night before and allow them to dry out overnight. However, if time is a factor, you can speed up the process by baking the cubes in a preheated 200°F (100°C) oven, turning once, for 20 to 30 minutes, or until dry.

● **Slow cooker size: 5 to 6 quart**

⅓ cup	melted butter or margarine, divided	75 mL
16 cups	day-old French bread cubes, lightly packed (see tip, at left)	4 L
1 cup	golden raisins	250 mL
3	eggs	3
1½ cups	granulated sugar	375 mL
2 tbsp	vanilla	25 mL
1 tsp	ground nutmeg	5 mL
1 tsp	ground cinnamon	5 mL
3 cups	milk	750 mL

Rum Sauce

½ cup	packed brown sugar	125 mL
2 tbsp	all-purpose flour	25 mL
¼ tsp	salt	1 mL
1 cup	water	250 mL
½ tsp	vanilla	2 mL
2 tbsp	dark or amber rum	25 mL

Lazy Cream

1 cup	whipping (35%) cream	250 mL
3 tbsp	confectioner's (icing) sugar	45 mL
2 tbsp	light or regular sour cream	25 mL
1 tsp	vanilla	5 mL

1. Brush 2 tbsp (25 mL) of the melted butter on bottom and up the sides of slow cooker stoneware. Layer bread cubes and raisins in slow cooker.

2. In a large bowl, beat together eggs and granulated sugar until thickened and lemon-yellow colored. Add vanilla, nutmeg, cinnamon, milk and remaining ¼ cup (50 mL) butter; beat for 1 minute longer to combine. Pour mixture evenly over bread, pressing down on cubes to saturate.

3. Cover and cook on **Low** for 6 to 7 hours or on **High** for 3 to 4 hours, until golden brown and slightly puffed. Allow pudding to cool slightly before serving.

4. *Rum sauce:* In a saucepan over medium-high heat, mix together brown sugar, flour and salt (this will avoid any lumps). Stir in water and vanilla. Bring mixture to a boil; reduce heat and simmer, stirring constantly, until mixture thickens. Stir in rum.

5. *Lazy cream:* In a bowl, with an electric mixer, combine whipping cream, confectioner's sugar, sour cream and vanilla. Beat until soft peaks form (do not overbeat). Cover tightly and refrigerate until ready to serve.

6. To serve, pour warm rum sauce into bottom of serving dish. Spoon warm pudding over top and dollop with lazy cream.

Tip

Removing lid of slow cooker releases heat, which will lengthen the cooking time. Do not remove lid until minimum cooking time.

Very Adult Rice Pudding

This is true comfort food — rich, satisfying and oh-so creamy.

• • •

Tip

If using rum, make sure it's the dark type. White rum will give this dish an unpleasant metallic flavor.

Make Ahead

This dish is best made the day before to give the flavors the opportunity to blend and develop.

• Slow cooker size: 3½ to 4 quart

1	can (13 oz/385 mL) evaporated milk	1
2 tbsp	packed brown sugar	25 mL
3 tbsp	butter, melted	45 mL
1 tsp	vanilla	5 mL
1	egg, lightly beaten	1
1 tsp	freshly squeezed lemon juice	5 mL
½ cup	dried cranberries or cherries	125 mL
2 cups	cooked rice (about ⅔ cup/150 mL uncooked)	500 mL
¼ tsp	ground cinnamon	1 mL
	Grand Marnier, amaretto liqueur or dark rum	
	Whipped cream	

1. In a bowl, combine milk, brown sugar, butter, vanilla, egg, lemon juice and cranberries, mixing well.

2. Place rice in lightly greased slow cooker stoneware. Pour milk mixture over rice and sprinkle with cinnamon.

3. Cover and cook on **High** for 2 hours (do not cook for a longer time on **Low**), or until top is set and a toothpick inserted in the center of the pudding comes out clean.

4. Spoon into serving bowls, drizzle with Grand Marnier and top with a dollop of whipped cream.

Library and Archives Canada Cataloguing in Publication

Pye, Donna-Marie
300 slow cooker favorites / Donna-Marie Pye.

Includes index.
ISBN 978-0-7788-0167-2

1. Electric cookery, Slow. I. Title. II. Title: Three hundred slow cooker favorites.

TX827.P934 2007   641.5'884   C2007-902980-9

Index

H

ham
    Basque Chicken, 219
    Bean and Beer Soup, Old
        World, 106
    Black Bean Cassoulet Soup,
        104
    Clubhouse Chicken, 218
    Easy Jambalaya, 142
    Ham and Lentil Ragoût, 132
    I'd-Swear-It-Was-Pizza Soup
        (variation), 97
    Slow-Cooked Macaroni and
        Cheese (variation), 186
    Slow Cooker Cottage Roll,
        295
    Spinach Turkey Rolls, 235
Harvest Corn Chowder with
    Bacon and Cheddar, 76
Hawaiian Pork Stew, 140
Hearty Beef Goulash, 98
Hearty Veal Stew with Red
    Wine and Sweet Peppers,
    130
Hearty Vegetarian Chili, 147
herbs, 15
Homestyle Pot Roast, 245
honey
    Chicken in Honey-Mustard
        Sauce, 212
    Country-Style Honey Garlic
        Ribs, 291
    Good Morning Granola, 28
    Honey and Spice Glazed Pork
        Chops, 285
    Honey-Lemon Beets, 311
    Honey-Orange Braised
        Carrots, 314
    Honey-Orange Crème
        Caramel, 350
    Steamed Pumpkin Date
        Cornbread, 35
Horseradish Mashed Potatoes,
    255
Hot Buttered Rum, 40
Hot Corn Dip, 56
Hot Crab, Artichoke and
    Jalapeño Spread, 61

Hot 'n' Spicy Winter Punch, 43
Hungarian Pork Goulash, 137

I

I'd-Swear-It-Was-Pizza Soup, 97
Italian Meatball and Bean
    Ragoût, 134
Italian Sausage and Tortellini
    Soup, 101
Italian Stuffed Peppers, 277

J

Jamaican Jerk Shredded
    Chicken Sandwiches, 231
jams and jellies (as ingredient)
    Caramelized Onion Chicken,
        217
    Corned Beef and Veggies with
        Marmalade-Mustard Glaze,
        St. Paddy's, 250
    Fruity Glazed Meatballs, 49
    Oxford Beef with Mushrooms,
        259
    PBJ Chicken Stew, 113
    Peking Pork Bites, 54
    Slow Cooker-to-Grill Sticky
        Ribs, 294
Johnnycake Cornbread, 34
Just-Like-Refried Frijoles Dip, 59

K

Key West Ribs, 292
Kids' Favorite Tuna Noodle
    Casserole, 188

L

lamb
    Calcutta Lamb Curry, 304
    Greek Lamb Loaf with
        Tzatziki Sauce, 307
    Lamb Shanks with Braised
        Beans, 302
    Rosemary and Garlic Leg of
        Lamb, 306
    South African Lamb Stew, 143

leeks
    Chicken-in-a-Pot, 210
    Easy Bean and Barley Soup,
        107
    Potato-Leek Soup with Stilton,
        85
    Royal Chicken Soup, 89
    Scalloped Sweet Potatoes and
        Parsnips, 321
    Tuscan Pepper and Bean
        Soup, 179
lemon
    Baked Lemon Sponge, 352
    Carrot Marmalade Pudding
        with Lemon Sauce, 358
    Lemony Herbed Drumsticks,
        214
    Old-Fashioned Gingerbread
        with Lemon Sauce, 334
    Osso Buco with Lemon
        Gremolata, 278
lemonade (frozen concentrate)
    Mulled Raspberry Tea, 37
    Tangy Winterberry Warmers,
        42
lentils
    Barbecued Veggie Joes, 200
    Ham and Lentil Ragoût, 132
    Lentil Curry with Squash and
        Cashews, 194
    Middle Eastern Pilaf, 327
    Spicy Vegetable-Lentil Soup,
        180
lettuce
    BLT Soup, 100
    Double-Decker Spicy Pork
        Tacos, 299
lime
    Almond-Pear Steamed
        Pudding with Coconut-
        Lime Sauce, 354
    Key West Ribs, 292
    Southwestern Pumpkin Soup,
        82
    Spicy Sweet Potato Soup, 86
liqueurs
    Amaretti Pear Crisp, 341
    Apricot Croissant Pudding
        with Caramel Sauce, 360

More Great Books from Robert Rose

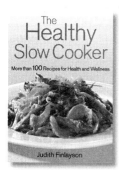

Appliance Cooking

- 125 Best Microwave Oven Recipes
  by Johanna Burkhard
- The Blender Bible
  by Andrew Chase and Nicole Young
- The Mixer Bible
  by Meredith Deeds and Carla Snyder
- The 150 Best Slow Cooker Recipes
  by Judith Finlayson
- Delicious & Dependable Slow Cooker Recipes
  by Judith Finlayson
- 125 Best Vegetarian Slow Cooker Recipes
  by Judith Finlayson
- The Healthy Slow Cooker
  by Judith Finlayson
- 125 Best Rotisserie Oven Recipes
  by Judith Finlayson
- 125 Best Food Processor Recipes
  by George Geary
- The Best Family Slow Cooker Recipes
  by Donna-Marie Pye
- The Best Convection Oven Cookbook
  by Linda Stephen
- 250 Best American Bread Machine Baking Recipes
  by Donna Washburn and Heather Butt
- 250 Best Canadian Bread Machine Baking Recipes
  by Donna Washburn and Heather Butt

Baking

- 250 Best Cakes & Pies
  by Esther Brody
- 500 Best Cookies, Bars & Squares
  by Esther Brody
- 500 Best Muffin Recipes
  by Esther Brody
- 125 Best Cheesecake Recipes
  by George Geary
- 125 Best Chocolate Recipes
  by Julie Hasson
- 125 Best Chocolate Chip Recipes
  by Julie Hasson
- 125 Best Cupcake Recipes
  by Julie Hasson
- Complete Cake Mix Magic
  by Jill Snider

Healthy Cooking

- 125 Best Vegetarian Recipes
  by Byron Ayanoglu with contributions from Algis Kemezys
- America's Best Cookbook for Kids with Diabetes
  by Colleen Bartley
- Canada's Best Cookbook for Kids with Diabetes
  by Colleen Bartley
- The Juicing Bible
  by Pat Crocker and Susan Eagles
- The Smoothies Bible
  by Pat Crocker

- 125 Best Vegan Recipes
  by Maxine Effenson Chuck and Beth Gurney
- 200 Best Lactose-Free Recipes
  by Jan Main
- 500 Best Healthy Recipes
  Edited by Lynn Roblin, RD
- 125 Best Gluten-Free Recipes
  by Donna Washburn and Heather Butt
- The Best Gluten-Free Family Cookbook
  by Donna Washburn and Heather Butt
- America's Everyday Diabetes Cookbook
  Edited by Katherine E. Younker, MBA, RD
- Canada's Everyday Diabetes Choice Recipes
  Edited by Katherine E. Younker, MBA, RD
- America's Complete Diabetes Cookbook
  Edited by Katherine E. Younker, MBA, RD
- Canada's Complete Diabetes Cookbook
  Edited by Katherine E. Younker, MBA, RD

Recent Bestsellers

- 125 Best Soup Recipes
  by Marylin Crowley and Joan Mackie
- The Convenience Cook
  by Judith Finlayson
- 125 Best Ice Cream Recipes
  by Marilyn Linton and Tanya Linton

- Easy Indian Cooking
  by Suneeta Vaswani
- Baby Blender Food
  by Nicole Young
- Simply Thai Cooking
  by Wandee Young and Byron Ayanoglu

Health

- The Complete Natural Medicine Guide to the 50 Most Common Medicinal Herbs
  by Dr. Heather Boon, B.Sc.Phm., Ph.D., and Michael Smith, B.Pharm, M.R.Pharm.S., ND
- The Complete Natural Medicine Guide to Breast Cancer
  by Sat Dharam Kaur, ND
- Better Food for Pregnancy
  by Daina Kalnins, MSc, RD, and Joanne Saab, RD
- Help for Eating Disorders
  by Dr. Debra Katzman, MD, FRCP(C), and Dr. Leora Pinhas, MD
- The Complete Doctor's Healthy Back Bible
  by Dr. Stephen Reed, MD, and Penny Kendall-Reed, MSc, ND, with Dr. Michael Ford, MD, FRCSC, and Dr. Charles Gregory, MD, ChB, FRCP(C)
- Crohn's & Colitis
  by Dr. A. Hillary Steinhart, MD, MSc, FRCP(C)
- Chronic Heartburn
  by Barbara E. Wendland, MSc, RD, and Lisa Marie Ruffolo